yarns
to DYE for

yarns
to DYE for

CREATING
SELF-PATTERNING
YARNS FOR
KNITTING

KATHLEEN
TAYLOR

 INTERWEAVE PRESS
www.interweave.com

Editor: Ivy Bigelow
Technical editor: Lori Gayle
Designer: Paulette Livers
Production: Samantha Thaler
Photo stylist: Paulette Livers
Illustrator: Gayle Ford
Photographer: Joe Coca
Proofreader and indexer: Nancy Arndt

 Interweave Press, Inc.
201 East Fourth Street
Loveland, Colorado 80537-5655 USA
www.interweave.com

Printed in China through Asia Pacific Offset

Library of Congress Cataloging-in-Publication Data

Taylor, Kathleen, 1953-
   Yarns to dye for : creating self-patterning knitting yarns /
Kathleen Taylor.
      p. cm.
   Includes index.
   ISBN 1-931499-81-0
   1. Dyes and dyeing--Textile fibers. 2. Knitting--Patterns. 3.
Yarn. I. Title.

10 9 8 7 6 5 4 3 2 1

Contents

7   Introduction

SECTION 1 PRINCIPLES

8   Chapter 1 *First Things First*

14 Chapter 2 *Materials*

18 Chapter 3 *Dyeing at Last*

SECTION 2 PROJECTS

30 Chapter 4 *Graduated-Color-Band Projects*

32   Cute as a Button!

36   Winter Frost Hat and Mittens

39   Autumn Sparkle Mittens, Headband, and Scarf

42   Wine-Stained Cables Hat and Scarf

45   School's Out Summer Shell

48 Chapter 5 *Zigzag Projects*

50   Cool Blues Summer Shell

53   Garden Colors Pillow Tops

56   Harbor Lights Leg Warmer Set

58 Chapter 6 *Striping Projects*

60   Child's Watermelon Sweater and Socks

64   Ladies' Watermelon Socks

66   Autumn Stripes Socks

68   Spring Stripes Socks

70 Chapter 7 *Fair Isle Projects*

72   Forest Trail Socks

74   Midnight Garden Socks

76   No-Slip Slipper Socks

80   Keyhole Scarf

82   Tassel-Top Earflap Hats

84   Wee Winter Mittens

86   Asymmetrical Vest

91   Carnival Colors Fingerless Gloves

93   Carnival Colors Gloves

96   Carnival Colors Wristbands

SECTION 3 USEFUL INFORMATION

98   Resources for Yarns and Dyes

98   Abbreviations List

99   Glossary

101   Index

This book is for new knitter
Melanie Reuter.
I'm sorry, EM, the yarn thing
is all my fault.

Acknowledgments

The Internet had a great deal to do with the creation of this book. A chance e-mail from Dr. Maggie set it all in motion. Another Internet friend, Ellen Hall, helped enormously by providing extra dye bottles. At Interweave Press, Betsy Armstrong, Paulette Livers, and Ivy Bigelow were always available online, and my agent Stacey Glick kept me grounded and informed throughout. Shirley McDermott and Ann Hilgeman have put up with me online for years, and I wouldn't get through a day without them. In the real world, the members of Knitters Etc. keep me in stitches every month, and, as always, Terry, with his graceful acceptance of wet yarn hanging all around the house, made the whole thing possible.

Introduction

I love self-patterning yarns. I love the ease of knitting complex-looking patterns without cutting and tying yarns. I love the seemingly endless combinations of bright colors. And I especially love the drawer full of socks I get to make after a buying binge. But socks aren't the only things I want to make, and fingering-weight yarn isn't the only yarn I want to work with.

I realized early on that if I wanted to use self-patterning yarns for projects that required bigger yarn or needles, I would have to figure out how to dye them myself.

So I did.

Though it took a bit of time to work out the process, dyeing self-patterning yarns at home was easier, and more fun, than I ever imagined it could be. This book is the result of those experiments. I hope you enjoy the journey as much as I did.

Chapter 1

First Things First

I know, I know. You've looked at the pictures, your needles are calling, and you're itching to get started. We'll get to that soon, but there are some things you need to know, and to think through, before you get out the dyes.

How Do Self-Patterning Yarns Work, Anyway?

Most commercially produced self-patterning yarns knit up into beautiful combinations of stripes, bands, or pseudo-Fair Isle patterns that repeat at regular intervals, but these are not the only kind of self-patterning yarns available. Many variegated yarns look like they're randomly dyed but in fact knit up into a zigzag effect that will repeat as long as the stitch number does not change. There are also yarns whose color repeat involves the entire skein; bands of color gradually shift and change throughout the items knitted with these.

Self-patterning yarns create an illusion; they are a dyer's trick. The patterns that develop in your knitting—whether they're stripes, spots that resemble Fair Isle, zigzagging areas of color, or gradually changing color bands—appear automatically because individually colored lengths of yarn are carefully spaced to knit into one or more colored stitches in a row or round. Colored stitches in successive rows or rounds overlap to create the patterns you see.

To get a sense of how the colored lengths in a self-patterning yarn create patterns, let's take an example. Say

Socks knitted with commercially produced self-patterning yarns. From left: zizag, graduated color-band, and striping/Fair Isle patterns.

you find that in knitting a sock you use just about one yard (.9 m) of yarn per round. A self-patterning yarn with a continuous, dyed-red section of ten yards (9 m) will knit up into a sock with a red band that goes all the way around the sock for about ten rounds. If you knit each round with the same yarn and needles but fewer stitches, the red band will widen because each round will use less yarn. If you knit with the same number of stitches per round but with larger needles, the red band will narrow because each round will use more yarn. For a self-striping project, a **band depth**—the number of rows or rounds that can be completed before the yarn changes color—can be predicted by dividing the length of the yarn dyed in the band's color by the length of the yarn it takes to complete a full round or row.

But what if you were to greatly increase the number of stitches per round, using our example yarn to knit, say, a sweater? The red band would be reduced to a narrow stripe. It might even be reduced to a partial stripe because the red section wouldn't be long enough to complete a full round. Even though the sweater would be knitted with the same yarn, at the same gauge, a viewer might see the red section only as variegation (or, if red sections overlapped, as part of a zigzagging pattern of red splotches). The red-dyed section in the yarn would need to be made much longer in order to create a recognizable red stripe.

Self-patterning yarns whose patterns repeat (that is, they knit up into repeating stripes, Fair Isle designs, or zigzags) are painted with dye all the way through the strands of a skein, so that when the skein is unwrapped, each wrap shows the same color pattern. Commercially produced self-patterning yarns are skeined in factories that can handle extremely long skeins. Long skeins allow room for pattern repeats with lengthy design elements (like long stretches of yarn in one color, such as red). The long design elements mean that nearly every knitting project, from an item with ten stitches per row to one with one hundred or more, will work up into a well-defined pattern, even though the band depths of its design elements may change.

Winding Yarn for Dyeing at Home
Okay, What About Those Big Skeins?

Most of us at home won't be able to handle skeins that are as long as commercially produced ones. But, to achieve self-patterning yarns that will stripe, zigzag, or emulate Fair Isle in our projects, we do need to wind and dye skeins that are much longer than the hanks of sixty-inch (1.5-m) circumference made by most skein winders or niddy-noddies. My default circumference for a skein (the default **skein length**) is forty feet (12 m). I did a lot of experimenting with different skein lengths, from a ten-foot (3-m) skein, wrapped around the footboard of my bed, to an eighty-foot (24-m) skein, wrapped around nearly every object in my house, before I settled on forty feet (12 m).

A forty-foot (12-m) skein is long enough to create a distinct pattern repeat that gives plenty of pattern variation and visual interest. Forty feet (12 m) is also a manageable length for skeining, tying, dyeing, and winding into balls.

Of course, that doesn't mean that skein lengths of thirty-seven feet (11 m), or forty-five feet (14 m), or twenty-nine (9 m) won't work. There are no right or wrong skein lengths. You'll need the same amount of yarn for any

given project regardless of the size of the skein. Using a short skein just means you'll have less space for design elements. As you knit, you'll have more pattern repeats per skein, so you will need fewer design elements or design elements that produce smaller band depths. A long skein means more space for design elements. As you knit, you'll have room for more, or longer, design elements. Flexibility and adaptation are the keys.

While you can use a skein as small as six feet (2 m)—half dyed in one color, half dyed in another—to make a narrowly striped two-color pattern, such a short pattern repeat is suitable only for small projects like socks or mittens. Items knitted with larger needles or with many more stitches per row won't show stripes all the way around, but will show short stripes or a zigzag effect, instead. Such effects are not necessarily a bad thing; you can use the yarn to advantage in large projects where striping isn't the object.

But if you want distinct stripes, especially if you're working on a project larger than a hat or with more than two colors, you'll need to wind skeins that are longer than six feet (2 m).

What Will I Wind the Yarn Around?

You can wind yarn around any two things that are far enough apart and that will hold steady while you wrap the yarn: doorknobs, fence posts, screws set in the wall, newel posts, or, as a last resort, patient family members. Kitchen chairs or other lightweight objects, unless they're firmly attached to the floor or wall, won't do because tension

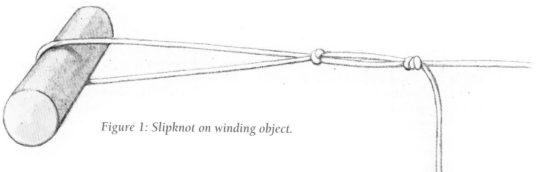

Figure 1: Slipknot on winding object.

on the yarn will change their positions. (Family members move, too—that is why they are a last-resort option.)

Make sure that these **winding objects** are out of the way of foot traffic, or wind yarn when you won't be interrupted by people needing to go around, under, or through the skein.

Winding the Skein

Select your winding objects, measure the distance between them, and multiply that distance by two. That will be the approximate circumference of the skein (the skein length). I say approximate because the tension you use to wind the yarn, and the yarn's own elasticity, can affect the length of the skein; moreover, the yarn will shrink after dyeing. For most of the projects in this book, you will want to achieve a skein length of about 40 feet (12 m). If your winding objects are only 10 feet (3 m) apart, you may want to reconsider your choice of them.

If the yarn you use is on a cone, already wound into balls (center pull or outside pull), or in commercial pull-skeins, you can begin wrapping. If the yarn is in a hank, you'll want to wind it into a ball first.

Begin by making a large slipknot in the yarn, leaving about a 15-inch (38-cm) tail. Tie the loop again with an overhand knot (so you're sure it won't slip out). Place the loop over the first winding object (see Figure 1).

String the yarn from the first winding object around the second winding object and back to the starting point.

Maintain enough tension to keep the yarn from sagging, but don't stretch it to the limit. Continue wrapping the yarn in this manner (yes, that means you'll be doing a lot of walking—wear comfortable shoes); keep the tension even. Wrap until you have wound enough yarn to complete your entire project. If you have to tie on more yarn, use an overhand knot and make sure that the ends are long enough to work into the knitting later. Bring the yarn back to the original loop and break it off, leaving about a 12-inch (30-cm) tail.

Loosely tie the rest of the skein with short lengths of waste yarn at about one-yard (1-m) intervals (see Figure 2).

Carefully slip the loop off the winding object (you'll have to pick up the rest of the yarn in order to do so because the loop will be underneath the rest of the wraps) and tie the loop firmly to the broken-off end of the yarn. Wrap the 12-inch (30-cm) tail around the skein twice and tie again. Don't tie the yarn too tightly because that will restrict dye absorption. Trim the excess tail and leave the loop to mark the beginning of the skein.

If you need more than sixty wraps for a project, you may want to make two skeins and dye them at the same time. Too much yarn in one skein may also restrict dye absorption.

When the skein is completely tied, carefully remove it from the winding objects. Try not to snarl or tangle the skein.

Figure 2: Skein tied, still on winding objects.

Not All Self-Patterning Yarns Require Long Skeins

Making up long skeins is a necessary part of dyeing yarns for zigzag, striping, and Fair Isle self-patterns. But in dyeing for graduated bands of color, an entire ball of yarn is immersed in a dyebath and slowly unwound and pulled from the dye. There is only one pattern repeat—the resultant yarn gradually changes color throughout the ball.

To knit a piece of fabric that also gradually changes color throughout, all the yarn required for the piece must be dyed at once. Once the yardage needed has been determined, simply wind the measured yarn into a ball (not a center-pull ball, which would be likely to tangle in being unwound from the dyebath). If you have to tie on additional yarn, use overhand knots, and make sure the tie-ends are long enough to be woven into the knitting later. The yarn should be wound loosely so that dye absorption is not restricted.

> ### *What if I discover that I don't have enough self-patterning yarn to complete a project?*
>
> • Dye more yarn, though you should be aware that dyelots rarely match perfectly.
> • Use solid-color, coordinating yarns (home-dyed or commercial) for ribbing, heels, toes, thumbs, sleeves, plackets, etc.
> • Use solid-colored or coordinating variegated textured yarn (mohair, bouclé, eyelash) to space out self-patterned sections.
> • Use self-patterning yarns as accent stripes in large pieces.
> • Strand self-patterning yarn with solid-colored yarn and use bigger needles.

The yardage you can dye in a single ball is limited by the size of your dyepot. I've learned that around 320 yards (292 m) is the maximum amount of most yarns that can be comfortably handled in a single ball at home. For large projects like sweaters you'll have to dye more than one ball, which means that your colors will gradually change from light to dark, and then back to light at the point where you attach the next ball of yarn. For matching items, like mittens that graduate in color across their entirety, you will need to dye a separate ball of yarn for each piece.

Several projects in this book call for solid-color yarns to complement self-patterning yarns. Those yarns can be wound into short skeins (with skein lengths of about 6 feet or 2 meters) on a niddy-noddy for dyeing. If you don't have a niddy-noddy, you can wind yarn around something similarly sized, like the back or the legs of a chair. These short skeins should be tied loosely with waste yarn in at least four places to prevent tangling.

How Do I Get Those Wonderful Patterns on the Yarn?

Stripe and zigzag yarns are made by laying out the long skeins just described and solidly handpainting measured sections of yarn with dye. Fair Isle designs are achieved by painting smaller dashes of dye on the yarn. Solid-color yarns and yarns with graduated color bands are dyed by immersing the yarn in a dyepot. Dyeing methods are described in depth in Chapter Three.

Is Self-Patterning Yarn Perfect?

Mostly. When you knit stripes or Fair Isle patterns in the usual way, you add a new color at the beginning of a row, or in a precise location dictated by a graph. All the pattern sections and elements line up perfectly in the finished piece. From a short distance, the individual elements in items knitted with self-patterning yarns look precise, but close inspection will reveal that stripes of color change in the middles of rows, that Fair Isle "dots" rarely line up with each other, and that matching pairs are hardly ever exact matches.

That is the nature of the beast. No matter how carefully you dye and knit, your pattern elements aren't going to line up perfectly. However, you can embrace the variations, enjoy the ease of knitting complex-looking patterns without having to change yarns, and take pride in the beauty of your work, knowing that you've created something unique.

How do I care for my home-dyed items?
- Store your home-dyed items as you would any handknit.
- Most yarns come with washing instructions—follow them.
- Assemble and block your projects as you would any other handknit.
- You can dry your home-dyed knits outdoors, but remember that sunlight can fade the colors.
- Wash your new home-dyed items separately—even well-rinsed yarn can bleed a bit in the first couple of washings.

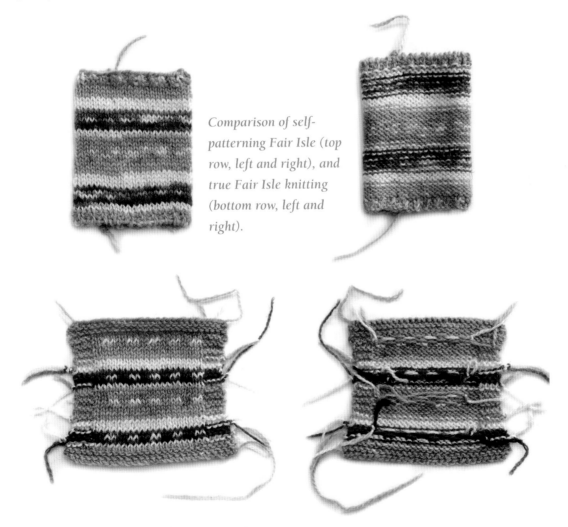

Comparison of self-patterning Fair Isle (top row, left and right), and true Fair Isle knitting (bottom row, left and right).

Chapter 2

Materials

Now that you have picked out some winding objects at home, you are going to need some other stuff. Let's start with the first thing you're likely to wonder about: dye. Many kinds of dyes are available to the home dyer, but we're concentrating on three brands of acid dye for the projects in this book. Don't let the word acid scare you—the acid we're talking about is plain white vinegar, the kind you buy in a grocery store.

In fact, you can get nearly everything you need to dye self-patterning yarns, including the dye, at the grocery store. The rest you can find at a yarn store, a dollar store, a thrift store, a rummage sale, or even in the collection already in your cupboards.

Dyes

Rit dye is a great dye for beginners; it's readily available, nontoxic, inexpensive, and it has a nice range of colors. It comes in both powder and liquid forms, which is handy. You should know that Rit is termed a *union dye,* since it is really two dyes mixed together. One dye colors cotton fiber; the other colors fleece fibers (wool, llama, alpaca, etc.), silk, and rayon. Each type of fiber will absorb only the dye formulated for it, so, unless you're dyeing yarn that is a blend of cotton and animal fibers or rayon, you're going to have residual dye left in your yarn. A potential draw-back to Rit is that residual dye; it may bleed if you're not very careful when you rinse a freshly dyed, heat-set skein.

Country Classics and **Gaywool** dyes are generally available at yarn and spinning shops, and they have wonderful color palettes. Both are easy to use, and both will color wool (llama, alpaca, angora, etc.), silk, and rayon yarns. The advantage to Country Classics and Gaywool dyes is that they are formulated only for the above-mentioned fibers, which means that the color will be absorbed completely. There is very little waste, and almost no chance of colors bleeding during the rinse. You must remember, though, that neither Country Classics nor Gaywool will dye cotton fibers, as Rit will.

None of our featured dyes will color acrylic fibers. And all yarns take dye differently. If possible, dye a small sample ball or skein of your yarn first to test the color absorption.

Yarn

In order to best re-create the projects in this book, you will want to use the yarn recommended in each pattern. When you begin to experiment, though, you should select a yarn that will both absorb the dye you intend to use and suit itself to your intended project. Smooth yarns are best for showing off Fair Isle patterning. Textured yarns, like brushed mohair, are fine for stripes and graduated-color-band projects. If you're a handspinner, you may want to give handspun yarns a try. Soft, superwash or shrink-resistant yarns are ideal for children's and baby items.

White and off-white yarns are obvious choices for dyeing, but I have overdyed gold, cream, peach, pink, yellow, and gray yarn with great success. Select light colors because intricate dye patterns won't show well over dark yarns.

Commercial yarn, especially yarn sold on cones, is often sized (treated with a gluelike coating to protect the yarn during the skeining process). Washing a small sample will remove the sizing and give you a better idea of the finished yarn's real texture, size, and elasticity.

In columns, from left: Rit, Gaywool, and Country Classic dyes.

Denim   Ivy   Desert Rose

Golden Yellow   Mustard   Kiwi

Tan   Nutmeg   Slate

Do Not Use Food Utensils for Dyeing.

This caution doesn't mean you have to spend a lot of money on bowls and storage containers. I use clean ice-cream buckets for rinsing and for microwave immersion dyeing, empty shampoo and dish soap bottles for storing leftover dye, and margarine and whipped-cream tubs for paint bowls.

The rest of the equipment is easy to assemble: wooden craft (Popsicle) sticks for stirring, large, zippered plastic bags (they need not be the highest quality), paper towels, a yardstick (plastic is nice since dyes stain wood), and heat-resistant plastic wrap. Double check to make sure that your plastic wrap is microwave-safe.

You'll also want a tablet and pen for jotting down the palette, recipe, and dye pattern you are using. Trust me, you won't remember later.

Equipment
New Things

Though all of our dye brands are nontoxic, you still need to mix and use them carefully. It is important to remember that dyes will color just about anything they come in contact with, including skin. Especially skin. So the first items on your equipment list are gloves.

It probably goes without saying that your gloves need to be waterproof. Hint: Many cheap disposable gloves, especially the transparent kind, aren't waterproof. After a cheap-glove fiasco, I settled on thin, latex gloves, like the ones used in the doctor's office. If you have a latex sensitivity, nonlatex synthetic gloves are available. You can find several varieties of gloves at grocery stores, drug stores, and discount stores. Wear gloves every time you handle dye, unless multicolored fingertips are your idea of a bold fashion statement.

You should also invest in a disposable dust mask to wear while you mix powdered dye. Although our recommended dyes are nontoxic, it's never a good idea to inhale dust.

You will need some foam paintbrushes in several sizes if you are planning to dye self-patterning stripe, Fair Isle, or zigzag designs. Buy an inexpensive multipack because you'll want one brush for each dye color used in each dye session. Though you can wash and reuse the brushes, you must always use a new brush for the lightest colors. No matter how well you rinse brushes, there is always enough residue to discolor yellow dye.

Purchase some measuring spoons, measuring cups, and a few long-handled spoons. Use plastic when possible—metal utensils can react adversely with dyes. Pick up a new set of spoons at a dollar store or thrift store; never use kitchen utensils with dye.

Things You Might Have on Hand

You probably already have the rest of the equipment, including a microwave or steamer for heat setting the dyed yarn (we will talk about that process in Chapter 3).

All dyes may stain clothing, tables, some floors, plastic utensils, and, once in a while, sinks (particularly old ceramic sinks and some new fiberglass sinks). If your sink isn't dye resistant, you may be able to very carefully funnel used dyebaths and rinsewater directly into the drain. You'll need old clothing or an apron, and you'll need protective coverings for your work surfaces.

I have a long trestle table set up for dyeing, though you can use your dining table or kitchen counter if you protect it. Cover your work surface with an old vinyl tablecloth or opened trash bags held in place with masking tape. I do my dyeing in a basement room where the concrete floor isn't harmed by the occasional spill. You should cover the floor of your work area with a drop cloth, especially if you are going to dye yarn in an area with wood flooring or carpeting. Vinyl flooring is more impervious to dye. Ditto ceramic tile, though grout isn't. In nice weather, working outside, in a shady area, is a great alternative.

No matter what kind of dye you use, do not use cooking utensils, bowls, or spoons for dyeing. You need dedicated utensils that will be used only for dyeing.

Materials Checklist:
- [ ] Dyes
- [ ] White vinegar
- [ ] Yarn
- [ ] Long table or counter for a workspace, plus a sink
- [ ] Large plastic funnel (if your sink isn't dye-resistant)
- [ ] Protective coverings for tables and floors
- [ ] Apron (or old clothes)
- [ ] Microwave or stovetop steamer
- [ ] Waterproof gloves
- [ ] Dust mask
- [ ] Foam paintbrushes (for striped, Fair Isle, and zigzag projects)
- [ ] Measuring spoons
- [ ] Measuring cups
- [ ] Long-handled spoons
- [ ] Wooden craft sticks
- [ ] Zippered plastic bags
- [ ] Microwave-safe plastic wrap
- [ ] Yardstick
- [ ] Assorted plastic buckets and bowls
- [ ] Paper towels
- [ ] Paper and pen

equipment

Chapter 3

Dyeing at Last

Only two methods are used to dye the yarn in this book: **handpainting** and **immersion.** Each method is easy to do, and each can be used to create an infinite variety of patterns and designs. Stripe, Fair Isle, and zigzag dye patterns are handpainted on long skeins of dry yarn. For solid colors (used to set off self-patterned portions of projects) and graduated-color-band designs, either wet or dry yarn is immersed in a dyebath.

Skeins—Long and Short

Most handpainted designs in this book call for a forty-foot (12-m) skein, but remember that you can adjust all the patterns to fit longer or shorter skeins by enlarging or reducing the number or size of the individual elements in your design. Short skeins are immersion-dyed to produce solid-colored yarns. Hand-wound balls are immersed in dye to produce graduated-color-band yarns. Read and refer to Chapter 1 for detailed instructions on skeining yarn.

General Handpainting Instructions

The preparation and general dyeing process is the same no matter which handpainted design (stripe, Fair Isle, or zigzag) you select.

Mixing the Dye

Most dyes come with manufacturer instructions, but our mixing methods may differ from theirs. We add vinegar to every dye mixture, we sometimes use cold leftover dye, and our mixtures often have a higher percentage of dye than manufacturers recommend.

Figure 3: Yarn skein on worktable, ready to be handpainted.

Here's how it's done (unless the pattern you choose specifies otherwise). Prepare one cup (240 ml) of very hot (not quite boiling) water. Measure 2 tablespoons (30 ml) of the hot water into the dye cup (8-ounce or 227-g plastic containers work perfectly). Add to the hot water ½ teaspoon (2.5 ml) of any powdered dye (or ¼ teaspoon [1.2 ml] of liquid Rit dye) and stir until the dye is dissolved. Add the remaining hot water and 2 tablespoons (30 ml) of white vinegar. Stir again.

Black dyes (no matter which brand) are the exception. Mix 1 full teaspoon (5 ml) of powdered dye per cup (240 ml) of water in order to produce a strong color.

The freshly mixed dye can be used immediately or poured into plastic bottles for storage. Use a permanent-ink marker to label each bottle with the dye brand and color name. If you have used a special recipe, note that on the bottle as well.

Don't be too alarmed if the mixed dye isn't the shade you expect. Many dyes only attain their final color after heat setting.

Preparing Your Worktable

Wind yarn into a skein, following the instructions in Chapter 1. Assemble your materials as in Chapter 2. Make sure your worktable is protected from dye spills and that you are wearing gloves and old clothes or an apron. Mix your dyes and place them on the worktable, along with a clean brush for each color.

Lay plastic wrap across your worktable. Locate the original slipknot loop—it marks the beginning of the skein. Place the beginning of the skein to the far left of the work surface and spread the dry yarn across the plastic wrap, keeping the strands as untangled as possible. You can allow what won't fit on the worktable to fall to the floor. Lay a yardstick above the yarn (see Figure 3).

20

Dip a foam brush into the first dye color and squeeze out the excess by pressing the brush on the edge of the cup. Carefully paint dye on the dry yarn, using the yardstick to measure out the length of yarn that needs to be painted in that color (see Figure 4). Dry yarn absorbs dye more slowly than wet yarn, giving you more control over color placement and minimizing unwanted color spread.

Some dry yarns absorb dye very quickly. Other dry yarns need more time, and more dye, before absorption takes place. In all cases, work slowly, with very little dye on your brush, until you become familiar with your yarn. To prevent mottling, make sure that all strands are evenly saturated (you may have to turn the strands over carefully to make sure that the dye has soaked through) but not sopping wet. If dye pools on or around the painted section, use paper towels to soak up the excess. The yarn should not drip when it is picked up or gently squeezed.

If you accidentally drip dye where it isn't supposed to go, use paper towels to soak up as much of the unwanted color as possible. Try not to worry too much about small spots and minor color spreading. Accidental spots often just add visual interest.

After you've painted a section of yarn, fold it carefully in the plastic wrap (see Figure 5). Wrapping the handpainted section preserves moisture for the heat-setting stage, and it keeps dye from bleeding onto other sections. Put the wrapped section aside. With paper towels, wipe the worktable completely to minimize color contamination. Spread out a new layer of plastic wrap, then the next length of yarn, and continue handpainting, folding each section in plastic and wiping the surface as you go along.

Once the entire skein has been painted, it is ready for heat setting.

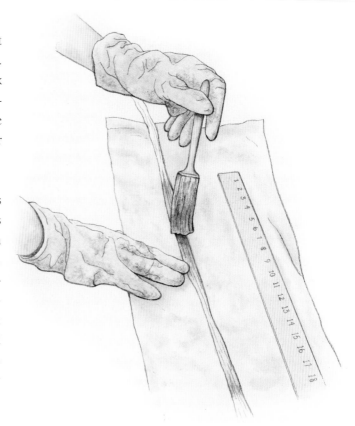

Figure 4: Handpainting.

Special Instructions for Stripe, Fair Isle, and Zigzag Designs

Most commercially produced self-patterning yarns feature a combination of stripes and Fair Isle sections. You can make yarns that are entirely striped or entirely Fair Isle.

Self-patterning **stripes** appear when enough yarn has been dyed in a solid color to complete one or more knitted rows or rounds. Handpainting stripes into self-patterning yarn is very easy; measure prescribed lengths of yarn on your skein and paint each section solidly with dye.

You can leave a half-inch (1.3-cm) space of undyed yarn between the colored sections. The dyes will wick toward each other during heat setting. If you don't mind a small

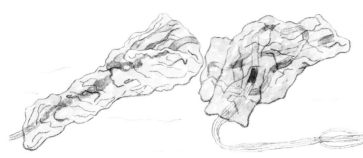

Figure 5: Sections set aside in plastic wrap.

area of blended color in your yarn, you can eliminate the space and let the dye sections touch.

Fair Isle self-patterning yarns are produced by dyeing short lengths (or *dashes*) of yarn at regular intervals. When the yarn is knitted up, just one or two stitches appear in the color of each dash. Those colored stitches line up in successive rows to form a pattern suggestive of Fair Isle knitting.

The spaces between the dashes can be left undyed or they can be handpainted with one or more dye colors after the first dyes have been heat set into the yarn. One-inch (2.5-cm) dashes show up in most of our projects as an area of color one or two stitches long. Two-inch (5-cm) dashes appear as an area of color three to five stitches long.

You can measure the spaces between the dashes by eye or by using your fingers or hands as guides. You can measure the spaces precisely, but the dye will wick a little in the heat-setting stage, so the final result will not be exact.

Because small areas of dye are prone to wicking, contrasting Fair Isle colors are painted in after the main colors of the skein have been dyed and heat set. The second dye stage works as follows: After the skein has cooled and has been rinsed, carefully paint the spaces between the already-dyed dashes. Wrap the newly painted sections in

plastic wrap and heat set the skein again. The rest of the skein need not be folded in plastic wrap for the last heat setting because those colors will not bleed or spread. Rinse the yarn, and it's ready to dry.

When **zigzag** patterns are knitted up, splotches of color appear to be randomly spread throughout the piece. But, in fact, zigzag self-patterning yarns do create a specific pattern repeat that can be seen when a knitted piece is examined closely. The splotches result from overlapping sections of yarn painted solidly with dye. These dyed sections are not long enough to complete a full row or round of knitting (as for a stripe), but not so short that they color only a few stitches (as for a Fair Isle effect).

Unlike striping yarns dyed at home, yarns dyed in a zigzag pattern are suitable for large projects such as adult sweaters. A forty-foot (12-m) skein may accommodate the dyed-section length necessary to create zigzags, but it would be impossible to dye sections long enough to create distinct stripes. The apparent randomness of the

Self-patterning stripes.

colored splotches in zigzag projects also has the advantage of disguising the color pooling that shows when a self-striping yarn is used and the number of live stitches changes greatly, as at the armholes.

As with striped designs, if your zigzag design uses colors that are similar in shade and intensity, you may paint the skein without leaving spaces between the individual color sections. A little wicking together of light blue and not-quite-as-light-purpley-blue will not hurt the pattern. If, however, your chosen zigzag design uses colors that do not blend well, you should leave a half-inch (1.3-cm) space of undyed yarn between the colored sections.

Immersion Dyeing for Graduated Bands of Color

Entire balls of yarn are dyed at once in graduated-color-band projects to produce just one color repeat—the yarn shades from light to dark, or from one light shade through several increasingly darker shades.

Before you begin dyeing a graduated-color-band project, you will need to wind the yarn into a loose, non-center-pull ball (see Chapter 1). In order to knit continuously shaded projects with matching pairs or multiple pieces,

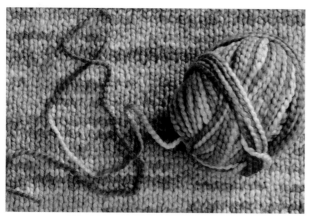

Self-patterning zigzags.

wind a ball of yarn with enough yardage for each portion (wind two balls for mittens, one ball for the front of a shell, and one for the back, etc.).

You will also need a waterproof niddy-noddy for winding the wet, dyed yarn into a skein. If you don't have a niddy-noddy, you may use the legs of an old chair or rig another system—just remember that the yarn is likely to stain whatever you wind it on.

From your assortment of plastic containers, select a large dyepot (I use a cleaned ice cream bucket). You will want just enough hot, but not boiling, water in this bucket to allow you, after you've added the mixed dye, to completely submerge the ball of yarn. It may be that you needn't add any hot water to the bucket—our project instructions give dye recipes that, alone, may fill the dyepot. You will also need to fill a rinse bucket (again, I use an ice cream bucket), with hot, but not boiling, water.

This is a messy process, so it's best to arrange the dyepot and rinse buckets in a dye-resistant sink. Be sure that the work area you choose is adequately protected from dye spills. Wear gloves.

Mix the primary dye with the vinegar and water, as per the instructions for the project, add the mixed dye to the hot water in the dyepot, and stir.

It is a good idea to dye a sample twenty-yard (18-m) ball of any yarn you intend to use, in order to see how quickly it absorbs dye and how long it takes for the entire ball to become saturated. A test ball will also tell you if your dyebath is strong enough to achieve the coloration you want. You may dilute or strengthen any dye recipe to suit your needs.

If the pattern directs, or if you wish to preserve the original color of the yarn at one end of the ball, unwind **reserve yarn** from the ball to be dyed. Loosely spool the reserved, undyed yarn near the rinse bucket, but not in the water. That yarn will remain undyed.

Immerse the dry ball of yarn in the dyebath. Push the yarn below the surface of the dye and hold it there for thirty seconds or so. Don't worry if the ball bobs back to the surface. It will sink when the yarn is completely saturated.

After thirty seconds have passed, lightly pinch the strand exiting the dyebath between a thumb and forefinger. With the other hand, pull about five yards (4.5 m) of yarn through your pinched fingers to remove excess dye liquid (the measurement need not be exact).

Allow the yarn you've just pulled from the ball to fall into the hot water in the rinse bucket. Don't push the yarn down, or move it around; just let it settle on its own (see Figure 6). And don't worry about a little color in the water of the rinse bucket; the yarn will retain its gradual color shading.

Wait another minute or two, then pull another five yards (4.5 m) from the dyepot, stripping out the excess dye as before. Drop this yarn into the rinse pot as before, allowing the yarn to drift on the surface until it sinks of its own accord.

Continue pulling lengths of yarn from the dyepot and stripping them of excess dye at regular intervals. You may decide on the length of those time intervals by observing how quickly the yarn absorbs the dye. Some yarns will absorb color very quickly; others will need a longer soaking period between each pull. Depending on how quickly the yarn absorbs dye, and how many yards are in the

Figure 6: Yarn pulled from ball in dyepot, pinched between thumb and forefinger, and settling in rinse bucket.

ball, the dyeing process could take anywhere from fifteen minutes to an hour or more to complete. Keep pulling the yarn and stripping the dye until almost all the yarn (except for any reserve yarn) is in the rinse bucket.

As you pull the yarn, it sometimes helps to give the ball in the dyepot a gentle squeeze to help the dye soak to the center. The center of the yarn ball will have the darkest color because it will have been in the dye the longest. When you've pulled all the way to the end of the yarn that has been at the center of the yarn ball, keep track of it by draping it over the edge of the rinse pot.

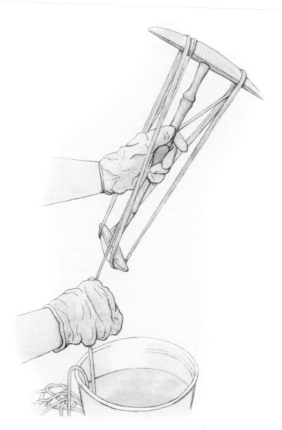

Figure 7: Yarn being wound on a niddy-noddy from the rinse bucket.

If the dyebath has not exhausted—that is, has not used up all the dye color (which it most likely will not)—you can set it aside and use it for immersion dyeing later. If you are dyeing more yarn in the same colorway, though, I suggest mixing a new dyebath so that your finished yarns will match as closely as possible.

Once the dyed yarn has been transferred to the rinse bucket, you can wind it into a skein for heat setting. Beginning with the dyed-yarn end that is hanging over the edge of the bucket, slowly and carefully wind the yarn on the niddy-noddy (see Figure 7). If you have not disturbed the yarn in the rinse bucket, you should be able to wind the yarn with a minimum of snarls and tangles. If you encounter tangles, slowly and carefully unsnarl

the yarn and continue winding. The last yarn wound on the niddy-noddy will be the undyed reserve yarn.

Secure the skein with four lengths of loosely tied waste yarn, as you would any other short skein. After tying, the yarn is ready for heat-setting.

Dyeing More Than One Ball at a Time

If you are dyeing yarn for a pair of mittens or socks, you'll want to dye two balls at once, using the method described above. If you have enough room in the dye-pot to submerge both balls, all you need is a rinse bucket for each ball of yarn. Pull and strip the yarn from one ball and then immediately repeat for the other, letting the freshly stripped yarns sink into individual rinse buckets. Allow an appropriate interval to pass, then repeat until the yarn from each ball has been dyed and is resting in a rinse bucket.

Winter Frost Hat and Mittens: a monochrome graduated-color-band project.

Monochrome and Multicolor Graduated-Band Dyeing

Monochrome graduated-color-band projects are usually dyed with just a single dye; the color gradually changes from one color at one end of the yarn to another color at the other end. This process can be used to fade one color into another—originally pink yarn can be made to shade to purple with blue dye, for example. Multicolor graduated-color-band projects use additional dye colors (sometimes these colors are added to the original dyebath, and sometimes new dyebaths are mixed) so that the yarn color changes in both intensity and tint (for example, yellow yarn can be made to gradually change to dark orange and then to red-orange).

Most monochrome color-band dyeing uses a single dye color. However, some patterns call for the addition of a small amount of mixed black dye near the end of the dyeing process as a "cheat" to deepen the final color. Our project instructions will indicate if and when black dye is to be added. You need not remove the soaking yarn

School's Out Summer Shell: a multicolor graduated-color-band project.

ball(s) from the dyebath in order to add the black dye. Simply move the ball(s) of yarn to the side, gently pour the mixed black dye into the dyepot, and stir. Some of the darker color may be absorbed unevenly into the surface layers of the yarn ball(s), but this will aid the effect of gradual color change.

Multicolor graduated-color-band dyeing is the same as monochrome band dyeing, except that additional dye colors are always added during the dyeing process. For projects in which the additional dye colors blend very well into the original dye colors (like dark orange to red-orange), add the additional colors as for the black dye mentioned above.

For multicolor projects in which the change of tint is more drastic (say, pale yellow to pale green to medium purple), additional dyebaths must be mixed. The pulling-and-stripping process remains the same, except that, at some point (or at several points), the dyepot is emptied and the yarn ball is immersed in a new dyebath. Be aware that some of the original dye will have bonded to the yarn in the ball—to radically change the tint, you will probably need to choose darker dye colors for subsequent dyebaths. If you avoid squeezing the ball of yarn in its original dyebath and/or wind the ball of yarn more tightly, so that less of the first dye soaks into the center of the ball, shifts of tint may be made distinct, even if you use dye colors that are about the same intensity.

Immersion Dyeing for Solid Colors

Solid-color yarns are dyed by another immersion process. The first step is winding all the yarn you need into a short skein, using a niddy-noddy or the back of a chair (see Chapter 1). For fast and even color absorption, soak the tied skein in warm water for at least half an hour. Immersion-dyeing dry yarn results in mottled or lightly variegated yarns. Some of our projects use that mottled look—the instructions will indicate if a solid-color yarn should be dyed dry.

Mix the dyebath according to the project instructions or the manufacturer's recommendations. For yarn amounts small enough to be completely submerged, you can mix the dye in a microwave-safe container like a clean ice cream bucket. For larger amounts of yarn, you will have to mix the dye in a large pot on the stovetop. You can use a pot from the thrift store, as the dyepot should never be used for cooking.

What if I don't like the colors?

Before knitting, you can wind the yarn into a small skein on a niddy-noddy or the back of a chair and overdye it by immersion, as you would for solid-color yarn. If you don't like the colors when the yarn has been knitted up, you can overdye the entire piece by immersion.

If you are microwave-dyeing, immerse the yarn in the dye and place the entire dyepot, covered with heat-proof plastic wrap, in the microwave. Cook on high for three two-minute intervals, with each heat cycle followed by a two-minute rest period.

If you are dyeing the yarn on the stovetop, bring the dyebath slowly to nearly a simmer. Immerse the yarn in the pot on the stove. Maintain the temperature for 15–20 minutes, then turn the heat off.

Allow the yarn and dyebath, whether you are stovetop- or microwave-dyeing, to cool to room temperature. The dye should be absorbed entirely by the yarn, leaving the dyebath clear, or nearly so. Pour off that clear dyebath, and you are ready to heat set and rinse the yarn.

Heat-Setting and Finishing

Heat-setting dyed yarn is a necessary step. Some dye colors need heat to achieve a final shade, and all of our dyes require heat-setting to make them permanent. The dye colors can run together if they are not heat-set quickly, even if the skein has been carefully wrapped. You may use the microwave or a stovetop steamer for heat-setting dyed yarns.

Heat-set your yarn immediately after you finish dyeing it.

Heat-Setting Yarn in the Microwave

Though there is no official prohibition against using the family microwave for dyeing yarns, ideally, you should set aside a separate microwave for the purpose. As always, we stress the use of dedicated tools and utensils. In any case, you will need large, microwave-safe, zippered plastic bags and potholders.

Place the skein of dyed yarn in a zippered plastic bag, and close the bag, leaving a one-inch (2.5-cm) opening to allow steam to escape. If the yarn was handpainted and wrapped in plastic, leave the plastic wrap on. If the yarn has dry areas between stripes or Fair Isle sections, add a teaspoon (5 ml) of water to the bag to aid in creating steam and to keep the dry yarn from burning.

Place the bagged yarn in the microwave and heat on high for two minutes. Then allow the yarn to rest, undisturbed, for two minutes. Repeat the heat/rest cycle twice.

Watch the yarn carefully to make sure it doesn't burn (take my word for it, smoldering alpaca produces a horrible stench). If the yarn gets too hot, reduce the heating to one-minute intervals and repeat the heat/rest cycles four times. You cannot salvage burned yarn.

After the last rest cycle, use potholders to carefully remove the bag from the microwave. Be aware that escaping steam can cause severe burns. Let the yarn cool, undisturbed, to room temperature. The dye continues to heat-set as the yarn cools; if you rinse the yarn too quickly, the colors will not be as vibrant, or as permanent, as they should be.

Zippered plastic bags can be reused several times before the zipper becomes too warped to close properly. Always check a used bag for residual dye. Discard discolored plastic, or use it only for heat-setting dark yarns.

Do not microwave dry yarn
Dry yarn can combust in the microwave. Always add a teaspoon (5 ml) of water to the zippered plastic bag if your yarn is partly dry. Do not close the bag completely or steam will cause the bag to pop.

Heat-Setting Yarn in a Steamer
As with all other dyeing tools and utensils, it's best not to use a steamer for food preparation after using it for dyeing.

You can steam more than one skein at a time. Though it is not absolutely necessary to put skeins in zippered plastic bags for steaming, bagging them will prevent color contamination and help keep the steamer clean. As for microwave dyeing, leave one inch (2.5 cm) of the zipper open to allow steam to escape. It is not necessary to add water to partly dry yarn if you are using steam to heat-set the dye.

To the steamer, add one or two inches (2.5 to 5 cm) of water and bring to a boil. Reduce the heat. Arrange the wrapped or bagged yarn on the steamer shelf and put the lid on. Allow the yarn to steam for twenty minutes. Peri-

odically check to make sure that the water has not boiled away. Add more as necessary.

After twenty minutes, turn the heat off and allow the yarn to cool to room temperature undisturbed.

Rinsing and Drying the Heat-Set Yarn
After heat-set yarn has cooled to room temperature, take it out of its plastic bag. If the yarn was also wrapped in plastic, you may remove and discard that.

Arrange the heat-set yarn on a sink edge. Turn the faucet(s) on and set the water temperature to lukewarm. For handpainted yarn, select one color section (it's a good idea to start with the darkest color), and hold it under the running water. Watch the water runoff for coloration. Some dye colors, and some dye brands, will not run at all, but others (especially red and black, and Rit dyes) will not have absorbed completely. The remaining colorant needs to be washed out. When the rinse water runs clear, gently squeeze the excess water from that dyed section (do not wring the yarn; that might stretch or felt it), set it aside (you can arrange it in a cleaned plastic container), and rinse the next color section. Continue to rinse each dyed section in this manner. When the entire skein has been rinsed in running water, soak it in clean water for ten minutes or so. Double check to make sure the rinse water is clear. If not, repeat the rinse. Be careful when you're handling the long, wet skeins so that the strands do not tangle.

Gently squeeze the water from the skein. You may carefully arrange the skein in a washing machine and set it to the spin cycle to remove excess moisture. Make sure that the washer does not spray water during its spin cycle, and remember to rinse out the washer before you do a load of laundry—run at least one entire, empty wash and

heat-setting and finishing

rinse cycle. If you don't have a washer, or if yours is not suited to spinning out the wet yarn, you can roll up the wet skein in an old towel to absorb moisture.

After excess moisture has been removed from the skein, it can be hung to dry over the backs of chairs (protect chairs by putting plastic wrap under the yarn), arranged on drying racks, or laid on the top of a washer until dry. Yarn can be hung outside in a breezy, shady area. Avoid bright sunlight because it can fade newly dyed yarn.

If you need to do a second stage dyeing session, allow the yarn to dry almost completely before painting the final dye sections (to minimize color wicking). Heat-set the second-stage dye as you did the first stage. Add water to the zippered plastic bag if you are heat-setting the new dye in the microwave.

If you are rinsing graduated-color-band yarn, or yarn that has been dyed a solid color, rinse the entire skein at once, spin (or roll the yarn in an old towel), and dry as instructed above.

Winding the Skeins into Balls
Wind the dry short skeins (from immersion-dyed yarns) into balls for knitting just as you would wind any commercial skein. A skein-winder or swift is handy for winding these short skeins, as is a ball winder. If you don't

Always dye enough yarn to complete your whole project because matching dye lots is impossible.
I learned the hard way that minimum yardage requirements sometimes fall short. Plus, when you use self-patterning yarns, there will be some waste if you make an effort to knit matching pairs or pieces. To be on the safe side, all the yardage requirements given for our projects allow for extra yarn.

have a swift and ball winder, you can easily arrange a dry skein over the back of a chair, carefully snip the ties, locate the end of the yarn, and wind the yarn into a ball by hand.

For graduated-color-band yarns, check which shade you want for the beginning of your knitting project. If you are winding a regular ball, begin winding the yarn at the opposite end of the yarn you want to begin knitting with (that is, if you want to begin knitting with the lightest color, begin by winding the darkest). If you are winding a center-pull ball (by hand or with a ball winder), begin with the shade you intend to knit first.

Long skeins (from handpainted yarns) will need to be placed on winding objects in order to be wound into balls. The dyed yarn is likely to have shrunk—sometimes up to three feet (1 m)—which means that you will not be able to put the yarn back on the original winding objects. (The yarn may also be considerably more elastic and fluffier than it was when you first skeined it.) I find that placing one end of the skein on a doorknob or other winding object, and the other end over the back of a kitchen chair, works well for holding the skein taut for winding into a ball.

Once the long skein is stretched taut, snip the ties very carefully. Snip only the ties, and not the skeined yarn (yes, I've done it, and no, I wasn't happy about it). Locate the beginning of the skein and snip off the original slipknot loop.

As for graduated-color-band yarns, decide which pattern element should appear first in your knitting. If you are winding a regular ball, begin with the other end of the yarn. If you are winding a center-pull ball, start with the end you want at the beginning of the project and wind from there. No matter which end you start with, you will have to walk back and forth between winding objects as you wind each wrap of the skein onto the ball.

If you are knitting socks or mittens, you can count the original number of wraps in the long skein, snip the yarn when half the wraps have been wound, and wind two identical balls so that you can knit both parts at once. Make sure that you begin winding both balls at the same point in the pattern repeat, and that you wind the yarn in the same direction.

Understanding Our Dye-Pattern Palettes

Instructions for our stripe, Fair Isle, and zigzag Dye-Pattern Palettes all use the same format. Each Dye-Pattern Palette lists the palette name, the dye style, the dye brand and colors used, special dye recipes, and specific dyeing instructions.

The measurements in the handpainted Dye-Pattern Palettes represent consecutive lengths of yarn to be painted with specific dye colors. If the Dye-Pattern Palette calls for a length of undyed yarn, measure off that portion and leave it unpainted.

Our graduated-color-band Dye-Pattern Palette will list the palette name, the dye brand and dye colors used, dye recipes, the amount of yarn needed for each piece, and the amount of undyed, reserve yarn (if any).

All dye amounts are given for powdered dyes.

Always remember that you can use our palette color suggestions and patterns to dye projects to match the ones shown in this book, or you can mix and match colors and pattern elements to invent your own unique yarns. Let your imagination reign.

Dye-Pattern Palette Fair Isle # 1

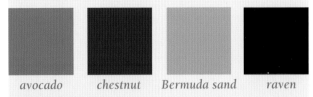

avocado   chestnut   Bermuda sand   raven

Dye Style Fair Isle.

Dyes Country Classics: avocado, chestnut, Bermuda sand, and raven.

Dye Recipes For each of the avocado, Bermuda sand, and chestnut dyes, mix ½ teaspoon (2.5 ml) dye with 2 tablespoons (30 ml) white vinegar and 1 cup (240 ml) hot water. Mix 1 teaspoon (5 ml) raven dye with 2 tablespoons (30 ml) white vinegar and 1 cup (240 ml) hot water.

Skein Length 40 feet (12 m).

First Dye Pattern Lengths 72" (183 cm) avocado; 72" (183 cm) avocado dashes 2" (5 cm) long and with 2" (5-cm) spaces in between; 72" (183 cm) Bermuda sand; 72" (183 cm) undyed; 36" (91.5 cm) chestnut; 72" (183 cm) chestnut dashes 2" (5 cm) long with 2" (5-cm) spaces in between; remainder undyed.

Second Dye Colors Mark the center of the avocado dashes section and paint the second half of those spaces with Bermuda sand. Mark the center of the chestnut dashes section and paint the second half of those spaces with raven.

Chapter 4

Graduated-Color-Band Projects

Some of the loveliest self-patterning yarns are also the most difficult to find ready-dyed. Graduated-color-band yarns may not be available at your favorite shop, but fortunately they are some of the easiest self-patterning yarns to dye at home. Beginning with white or colored yarns—fuzzy or smooth—you can dye simple graduations from one shade to another, or complex shifts from color to color. While graduated-color-band projects can be lovely plain, they provide an intriguing backdrop to embellishment and stitch-patterning, too. The projects in this chapter should give you an idea of the myriad directions you can take in dyeing and working with graduated-color-band yarns.

Cute as a Button!

Delight the little girl in your life with these playful chill-chasers! Originally pink yarn is dyed to graduate into purple; colorful buttons make the set even more fun. Begun with a white or green yarn, this dye pattern could work for boys' sets, too.

Finished Size *Hat:* 16 (18)" (40.5 [45.5] cm) head circumference and 6½ (7½)" (16.5 [19] cm) tall, not including tassels. *Mittens:* 6 (7)" (15 [18] cm) hand circumference and 6¾ (7½)" (17 [19] cm) long from base of cuff to tip. *Scarf:* 3" (7.5 cm) wide (with ribbing relaxed) and 39" (99 cm) long, not including tassels. To fit a small (large) child.

Yarn *Worsted-weight wool:* about 327 (436) yd (300 [400] m) pink. We used Cascade Yarns 109 Tweed LE (90% wool; 10% Donegal tweed; 109 [100 m]/100 g): #U608 hot pink, 3 (4) skeins.

Needles *Hat:* Size 9 (5.5 mm), set of 4 double-pointed (dpn). *Mittens:* Size 8 (5 mm), set of 4 dpn. *Scarf:* Size 10½ (6.5 mm), straight. Adjust needle size if necessary to obtain the correct gauge.

Notions Stitch markers (m); tapestry needle; 2 safety pins or 1 stitch holder; assorted colorful buttons; sewing needle and matching thread.

Gauge 15 sts and 23 rnds = 4" (10 cm) in St st worked in the round on size 9 (5.5 mm) needles; 17½ sts and 26 rows = 4" (10 cm) in St st worked in rows on size 8 (5 mm) needles in the round.

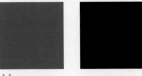

blue spruce   raven

Dye Style Monochrome Graduated-Band.

Dye Country Classics: blue spruce and raven.

Recipe Mix 1 teaspoon (5 ml) blue spruce dye with ¼ cup (60 ml) white vinegar and 9 cups (2 liters) hot water. Mix ½ teaspoon (2.5 ml) raven dye with 2 tablespoons (30 ml) water.

Special Dyeing Instructions Add mixed raven dye when ¼ of each yarn ball remains.

Yardage for Each Yarn Ball: *Hat:* 1 ball containing 109 (120) yd (100 [110] m). *Mittens:* 2 balls, each containing 50 yd (46 m). *Scarf:* 1 ball containing 109 yd (100 m).

Amount of Undyed Reserve Yarn *Hat:* 10 yd (9 m). *Mittens:* 5 yd (4.5 m) in each ball. *Scarf:* 10 yd (9 m).

Special Instructions Measure, cut, and save 9 yd (8 m) of yarn from the skein used for the mittens. This yarn remains undyed and will be used for half of the scarf tassels.

Yardage for Each Yarn Ball *Hat:* 1 ball containing 109 (120) yd (100 [110] m). *Mittens:* 2 balls, each containing 50 yd (46 m). *Scarf:* 1 ball containing 109 yd (100 m).

Hat

With size 9 (5.5 mm) dpn and beg at the light end of the dyed yarn, CO 60 (68) sts. Divide sts as evenly as possible on 3 dpn. Join for working in the rnd, and place marker (pm) to indicate beg of rnd (slip marker every rnd).

Next rnd: *K1, p1; rep from * around. Rep this rnd 3 more times. Change to St st (knit all sts every rnd) and work even until piece measures 6½ (7½)" (16.5 [19] cm) from beg. Divide sts evenly on 2 dpn. With WS touching and using the three-needle method (see Glossary, page 100), BO sts tog to form a decorative seam across the top.

I-Cord Tassels: With darkest yarn, work nine 2½" (6.5-cm) I-cord tassels evenly spaced across BO edge as foll: With size 9 (5.5 mm) dpn, pick up and knit 3 sts from BO edge of hat.

All rows: Without turning the work, slide all sts to right needle tip, bring yarn around behind the work, k3. Tug the finished sts gently to snug up the I-cord tube. Rep the last row until tassel measures about 2½" (6.5 cm) from pick-up row. To finish, k3tog—1 st rem. Cut yarn, leaving a 6" (15-cm) tail, and pull tail through last st to fasten off. Make eight more tassels across BO edge of hat in the same manner.

Finishing: Weave in ends. Draw the final tail of each I-cord tassel into the center of the I-cord, and trim the excess. Hand wash and block. Fold lower edge up 1" (2.5 cm) for brim. With sharp-pointed sewing needle and matching sewing thread, sew buttons, randomly placed, on the front of the hat.

Mittens *(make 2)*

Cuff: With size 8 (5 mm) dpn and beg at the light end of the dyed yarn, CO 26 (30) sts. Divide sts as evenly as possible on 3 dpn. Join for working in the rnd, and place marker (pm) to indicate beg of rnd (slip marker every rnd). *Next rnd:* *K1, p1; rep from * around. Rep this rnd 11 (14) more times—12 (15) rnds of ribbing completed; piece should measure about 2¼ (2¾)" (5.5 [7] cm) from beg.

Thumb gusset: Knit 3 (4) rnds even. Cont as foll:

Rnd 1: (Inc rnd) M1 (see Glossary, page 100), k1, M1, pm, knit to end—28 (32) sts total; 3 gusset sts between markers.

Rnd 2: Knit.

Rnd 3: (Inc rnd) M1, knit to next m, M1, slip marker, knit to end—2 gusset sts inc'd between markers.

Rnd 4: Knit.

Rep the last 2 rnds 2 (3) more times—34 (40) sts; 9 (11) gusset sts between markers.

Hand: Place the 9 (11) gusset sts on a stitch holder (or divide the sts on 2 safety pins to make it easier to try on the mitten) to work later for thumb. Using the backward loop method (see Glossary, page 98), CO 1 st over the gap, knit to end—26 (30) sts. Knit 6 (8) rnds even. Knit 1 rnd, dec 2 sts evenly spaced—24 (28) sts rem. *For the larger size only:* Work 2 rnds as foll: *K5, k2tog; rep from * around; then knit 1 rnd even—24 sts rem for both sizes.

Shape top: Cont for both sizes as foll:

Rnd 1: *K4, k2tog; rep from * around—20 sts rem.

Rnds 2, 4, and 6: Knit.

Rnd 3: *K3, k2tog; rep from * around—16 sts rem.

Rnd 5: *K2tog; rep from * around—8 sts rem.

Rnd 7: Rep Rnd 5—4 sts rem.

Cut yarn, leaving a 12" (30.5-cm) tail. Thread tail on tapestry needle and draw through rem sts. Pull snugly to close mitten tip, and fasten off on inside.

Thumb: Arrange the 9 (11) held gusset sts as evenly as possible on 3 dpn. Join yarn to end of sts with RS facing. Pick up and knit 1 st from the base of st CO over the gap in the hand, knit to end—10 (12) sts. Knit 4 (6) rnds even. *Next rnd:* *K2tog; rep from * around—5 (6) sts rem. Knit 1 rnd even. Cut yarn, leaving a 12" (30.5-cm) tail. Thread tail on tapestry needle and draw through rem sts. Pull snugly to close thumb tip, and fasten off on inside.

Finishing: Weave in ends. With sharp-pointed sewing needle and matching sewing thread, sew buttons, randomly placed, on the back of each mitten.

Scarf

With size 10½ (6.5 mm) straight needles and beg at light end of dyed yarn, CO 18 sts.

Row 1: *K2, p2; rep from * to last 2 sts, end k2.

Row 2: *P2, k2; rep from * to last 2 sts, end p2.

Rep Rows 1 and 2 until about 10 yd (9 m) of yarn remains. BO all sts loosely in rib patt.

I-Cord Tassels: Using the reserved undyed yarn for the lighter end and the rem darkest yarn for the darker end, make five 3½" (9-cm) I-cord tassels evenly spaced across each end of scarf as foll: Pick up and knit 3 sts from scarf edge. *All rows:* Without turning the work, slide the sts to right needle tip, bring yarn around behind the work, k3. Tug the finished sts gently to snug up the I-cord tube. Rep the last row until tassel measures about 3½" (9 cm) from pick-up row. To finish, k3tog—1 st rem. Cut yarn, leaving a 6" (15-cm) tail. Pull tail through last st to fasten off. Make four more tassels across scarf end in the same manner, then work five tassels at the opposite end.

Finishing: Weave in ends. Draw the final tail of each I-cord tassel into the center of the I-cord, and trim the excess. Hand wash and block. With sharp-pointed sewing needle and matching sewing thread, sew buttons, randomly placed, to the last few inches on the RS of each scarf end.

What kind of embellishments can I use on my finished pieces?
Let your imagination reign! Buttons, ribbons, sequins, appliqués, embroidery, or beads can turn your already-one-of-a-kind self-patterning projects into works of art.

cute as a button!

Winter Frost Hat and Mittens

Add the sparkling look of frost to your hat and mittens with strategically sewn iridescent pail-lettes and beads. This is a great pattern for your first graduated-band dyeing attempt because it takes advantage of just one dye color. It also shows just how surprising home-dyeing can be—that one dye color is black.

Finished Size Hat: 22½" (57 cm) head circumference and 7¾" (19.5 cm) tall. **Mittens:** 7½ (8¼)" (19 [21] cm) hand circumference and 9½ (10¾)" (24 [27.5] cm) long from base of cuff to tip. Hat to fit most adults; mittens to fit women's medium/large (men's medium).

Yarn *Worsted-weight wool:* about 327 yd (300 m) pale yellow. We used Cascade Yarns 109 Tweed LE (90% wool; 10% Donegal tweed; 109 yd [100 m]/100 g): #U626 maize, 3 skeins.

Needles Hat: Size 9 (5.5 mm), set of 4 double-pointed (dpn). **Mittens:** Size 8 (5 mm): set of 4 dpn. Adjust needle size if necessary to obtain the correct gauge.

Notions Stitch markers (m); tapestry needle; 2 safety pins or 1 stitch holder; 1 package 4-mm flat square paillettes in clear iridescent; 1 package rocaille beads in light gray iridescent; beading needle; matching sewing thread.
Note: Beads and pailettes available from craft and hobby shops; ours were obtained through Cartwright's Sequins (see Resources, page 98.)

Gauge 16 sts and 25 rnds = 4" (10 cm) in St st worked in the round on size 9 (5.5 mm) needles; 17½ sts and 26

raven

Dye Style Monochrome Graduated-Band.
Dye Country Classics: raven.
Dye Recipe Mix ⅛ teaspoon (0.6 ml) raven dye with ¼ cup (60 ml) white vinegar and 9 cups (2 liters) hot water.
Special Dyeing Instructions Add ¼ teaspoon (1.2 ml) raven dye mixed with 2 tablespoons (30 ml) of water to the dyebath when ⅓ of the yarn has been dyed. Add another ¼ teaspoon (1.2 ml) raven dye mixed with 2 tablespoons (30 ml) of water to the dye-bath when ⅔ of the yarn has been dyed.
Yardage for Each Yarn Ball Hat: 1 ball containing 140 yd (128 m). **Mittens:** 2 balls, each containing 50 yd (46 m).
Amount of Undyed Reserve Yarn Hat: 20 yd (18 m). **Mittens:** 10 yd (9 m).

rows = 4" (10 cm) in St st worked in the round on size 8 (5 mm) needles.

Hat

With size 9 (5.5 mm) dpn and beg at light end of the yarn, CO 90 sts. Divide sts evenly on 3 dpn. Join for working in the rnd and place marker (pm) to indicate beg of rnd (slip marker every rnd). *Next rnd:* *K1, p1; rep from * around. Rep this rnd 5 more times. Change to St st (knit all sts every rnd) and work even until piece measures 4¼" (11 cm) from beg.
Shape top: Cont as foll:
Rnd 1: *K7, k2tog: rep from * around—80 sts rem.
Rnds 2, 4, 6, 8, 10, 12, 14, and 16: Knit.
Rnd 3: *K6, k2tog: rep from * around—70 sts rem.

Rnd 5: *K5, k2tog; rep from * around—60 sts rem.

Rnd 7: *K4, k2tog; rep from * around—50 sts rem.

Rnd 9: *K3, k2tog; rep from * around—40 sts rem.

Rnd 11: *K2, k2tog; rep from * around—30 sts rem.

Rnd 13: *K1, k2tog; rep from * around—20 sts rem.

Rnd 15: *K2tog; rep from * around—10 sts rem.

Rnd 17: Rep Rnd 15—5 sts rem.

Cut yarn, leaving a 12" (30.5-cm) tail. Thread tail on a tapestry needle and draw through rem sts. Pull snugly to close top of hat, and fasten off on inside. Weave in ends.

Embellishments: Attach each paillette/bead combination as foll: Thread beading needle with sewing thread, bring the needle out to the RS of work from inside the hat, thread needle through a paillette, and then through a rocaille bead. Loop the thread back through the center of the paillette and tighten to anchor the bead to the top of the paillette. Bring the thread to the WS of the hat and work a knot on the inside to secure. Work a randomly spaced line of paillette/bead combinations around the hat just above the ribbing, as shown in photo. The crown of the hat has nine radiating decrease lines. Work a line of paillette/bead combinations along each decrease line, working from the base of the line to the top of the hat.

Mittens *(make 2)*

Cuff: With size 8 (5 mm) dpn and beg at light end of the dyed yarn, CO 32 (36) sts. Divide sts as evenly as possible on 3 dpn. Join for working in the rnd and place marker (pm) to indicate beg of rnd (slip marker every rnd). *Next rnd:* *K1, p1; rep from * around. Rep the last rnd 14 more times—15 rnds of ribbing completed; piece should measure about 2¾" (7 cm) from beg.

Thumb gusset: Knit 5 (7) rnds even. Cont as foll:

Rnd 1: (Inc rnd) M1 (see Glossary, page 100), k1, M1, pm, knit to end—34 (38) sts; 3 gusset sts between markers.

Rnd 2: Knit.

Rnd 3: (Inc rnd) M1, knit to next m, M1, slip marker, knit to end—2 sts inc'd between gusset markers.

Rnd 4: Knit.

Rep the last 2 rnds 3 (4) more times—42 (48) sts; 11 (13) gusset sts between markers.

Hand: Place the 11 (13) gusset sts on a stitch holder (or divide sts on 2 safety pins to make it easier to try on the mitten) to work later for thumb, use the backward loop method (see Glossary, page 99) to CO 1 st over the gap, knit to end—32 (36) sts. Knit 19 (23) rnds even, or until mitten reaches to tip of little finger. *For the smaller size only:* Knit 1 rnd while dec 2 sts evenly spaced, then knit 1 rnd even—30 sts rem. *For the larger size only:* *K4, k2tog; rep from * around, then knit 1 rnd even—30 sts rem for both sizes.

Shape top: Cont for both sizes as foll:

Rnd 1: *K3, k2tog; rep from * around—24 sts rem.

Rnds 2, 4, and 6: Knit.

Rnd 3: *K2, k2tog; rep from * around—18 sts rem.

Rnd 5: *K1, k2tog; rep from * around—12 sts rem.

Rnd 7: *K2tog; rep from * around—6 sts rem.

Cut yarn, leaving a 12" (30.5-cm) tail. Thread tail on tapestry needle and draw through rem sts. Pull snugly to close mitten tip, and fasten off on inside.

Thumb: Arrange 11 (13) held gusset sts as evenly as possible on 3 dpn. Join yarn to end of sts with RS facing. Pick up and knit 1 st from base of the st CO over the gap in the hand, knit to end—12 (14) sts. Knit 10 (12) rnds even. *Next rnd:* *K2tog; rep from * around—6 (7) sts rem. Knit 1 rnd even. *Next rnd:* *K2tog; rep from * around, ending k0 (1)—3 (4) sts rem. Cut yarn, leaving a 12" (30.5-cm) tail. Thread tail on tapestry needle and draw through rem sts. Pull snugly to close thumb tip, and fasten off on inside. Weave in ends.

Embellishments: Work randomly spaced lines of paillette/bead combinations on the back of each mitten as for hat, as foll: above the ribbing, at the base of the thumb, just below the beg of the hand decreases, and at the very top. Sew a few paillettes/beads to the back side of each thumb near the tip.

Autumn Sparkle Mittens, Headband, and Scarf

This fiery set sparkles with carry-along metallic thread, and it shows how well different yarns (a wool and a mohair blend) can look when they're dyed to match. As a bonus, the set is guaranteed to keep you warm on brisk days.

Finished Size *Mittens:* 7 (8)" (18 [20.5] cm) hand circumference and 9¾ (11)" (25 [28] cm) long from base of cuff to tip. *Headband:* 20 (21)" (51 [53.5] cm) head circumference and 2½" (6.5 cm) wide. *Scarf:* 4" (10 cm) wide, and 66" (167.5 cm) long. Mittens to fit women's small/medium (women's large/men's small); headband to fit adult small/medium (medium/large).

Yarn *Worsted-weight wool:* about 490 yd (448 m) yellow. We used Brown Sheep Nature Spun Worsted (100% wool; 245 yd [224 m]/100 g): #305 impasse yellow, 2 skeins total for mittens and headband. *Sportweight brushed mohair or*

Dye-Pattern Palette Multicolor #1

| pumpkin | butterscotch | rust | ripe tomato |

raven

Dye Style Multicolor Graduated-Band.

Dye Country Classics: pumpkin, butterscotch, rust, ripe tomato, and raven.

Dye Recipe Mix ½ teaspoon (2.5 ml) pumpkin dye with ¼ cup (60 ml) white vinegar and 9 cups (2 liters) hot water.

Special Dyeing Instructions Add ½ teaspoon (2.5 ml) butterscotch dye mixed with 2 tablespoons (30 ml) water to dyebath after ¼ of the yarn has been dyed. Add ½ teaspoon (2.5 ml) rust dye mixed with 2 tablespoons (30 ml) water to dyebath after ½ of the yarn has been dyed. Add ½ teaspoon (2.5 ml) ripe tomato dye mixed with 2 tablespoons (30 ml) water to dyebath after ¾ of the yarn has been dyed. Add ⅛ teaspoon (0.6 ml) raven dye mixed with 2 tablespoons (30 ml) water to dyebath when only a few yards of the yarn remain.

Yardage for Each Yarn Ball *Mittens and Headband:* 2 balls, each containing 245 yd (224 m) of the wool. *Scarf:* 1 ball containing 89 yd (81 m) of the mohair blend.

Amount of Undyed Reserve Yarn 10 yd (9 m) of each ball.

brushed mohair blend: about 89 yd (81 m) yellow. We used Ironstone Yarns English Mohair (78% mohair, 13% wool, 9% nylon; 89 yd [81 m]/40 g): #818 daffodil (yellow), 1 skein for scarf. *Metallic thread:* 350 yd (320 m) in a coordinating color. We used Kreinik Metallics Balger Cord (100% polyester metallic; 54 yd [50 m]/spool): #041C, 7 spools.

Needles Mittens and Headband: Size 8 (5 mm): set of 4 double-pointed (dpn). *Scarf:* Size 15 (10 mm): straight. Adjust needle size if necessary to obtain the correct gauge. *Notions* Stitch markers (m); tapestry needle; 2 safety pins or 1 stitch holder.

Gauge 20½ sts and 28 rnds = 4" (10 cm) in St st worked in the round on size 8 (5 mm) needles with Nature Spun Worsted and metallic thread held together; 10 sts and 14 rows = 4" (10 cm) in garter st worked in rows on size 15 (10 mm) needles with English Mohair and metallic thread held together.

Note: All pieces are worked with one strand of yarn and one strand of metallic thread held together throughout.

Mittens *(make 2)*

With size 8 (5 mm) dpn, beg at light end of the dyed Nature Spun Worsted yarn, and holding wool yarn and metallic thread tog, CO 36 (40) sts. Divide sts as evenly as possible on 3 dpn. Join for working in the rnd and place marker (pm) to indicate beg of rnd (slip marker every rnd). *Next rnd:* *K1, p1; rep from * around. Rep this rnd 14 more times—15 rnds of ribbing completed; piece should measure about 3" (7.5 cm) from beg.

Thumb gusset: Knit 5 (7) rnds even. Inc for gusset as foll:

Rnd 1: (Inc rnd) M1 (see Glossary, page 100), k1, M1, pm, knit to end—38 (42) sts; 3 gusset sts between markers.

Rnd 2: Knit.

Rnd 3: (Inc rnd) M1, knit to next m, M1, slip marker, knit to end—2 sts inc'd between markers.

Rnd 4: Knit.

Rep the last 2 rnds 4 (5) more times—48 (54) sts; 13 (15) gusset sts between markers.

Hand: Place 13 (15) gusset sts on a stitch holder (or divide sts on 2 safety pins to make it easier to try on the mitten) to work later for thumb, use the backward loop method (see Glossary, page 99) to CO 1 st over the gap, knit to end—36 (40) sts. Knit 20 (22) rnds even, or until mitten reaches to tip of little finger. *For the larger size only:* Work 3 rnds as foll: Knit 1 rnd while dec 1 st on each of the 3 needles—37 sts rem; then knit 1 rnd even; then knit 1 rnd while dec 1 st—36 sts rem for both sizes.

Shape top: Cont for both sizes as foll:

Rnd 1: *K4, k2tog; rep from * around—30 sts rem.

Rnds 2, 4, 6, and 8: Knit.

Rnd 3: *K3, k2tog; rep from * around—24 sts rem.

Rnd 5: *K2, k2tog; rep from * around—18 sts rem.

Rnd 7: *K1, k2tog; rep from * around—12 sts rem.

Rnd 9: *K2tog; rep from * around—6 sts rem.

Cut yarn, leaving a 12" (30.5-cm) tail. Thread tail on tapestry needle and draw through rem sts. Pull snugly to close mitten tip, and fasten off on inside.

Thumb: Arrange 13 (15) held gusset sts as evenly as possible on 3 dpn. Join yarn to end of sts with RS facing. Pick up and knit 1 st from the base of the st CO over the gap in the hand, knit to end—14 (16) sts. Knit 9 (11) rnds even. *Next rnd:* *K2tog; rep from * around—7 (8) sts rem. Knit 1 rnd even. *Next rnd:* *K2tog; rep from * around, ending k1 (0)—4 sts rem. Cut yarn, leaving a 12" (30.5-cm) tail. Thread tail on tapestry needle and draw through rem sts. Pull snugly to close thumb tip, and fasten off on inside. Weave in ends.

Headband

With size 8 (5 mm) dpn, the darkest Nature Spun Worsted yarn leftover from mittens, and holding yarn and metallic thread tog, CO 24 sts. Divide sts evenly on 3 dpn. Join for working in the rnd and place marker (pm)

to indicate beg of rnd (slip marker every rnd). *Note:* The leftover yarn is likely to be all of the same shade; if some graduation is visible, begin with the darkest shade, break off yarn halfway through the knitting, and begin again with the lighter yarn of same shade from second leftover ball. Knit every rnd until piece measures 20 (21)" (51 [53.5] cm) from beg. BO all sts. With yarn threaded on a tapestry needle, sew CO and BO edges tog. Weave in ends. Flatten the tube into a band for wearing.

Scarf

With size 15 (10 mm) straight needles, beg at light end of the dyed English Mohair yarn, and holding yarn and metallic thread tog, CO 10 sts. Work in garter st (knit every st every row) until all but about 1 yd (1 m) of yarn has been used. BO all sts. Weave in ends.

What if the color changes in my graduated-color-band project come out too subtle? You can briefly dip the darker end of the knitted item in the darkest dye color used in the palette. Refer to the dye manufacturer's instructions for information on dyeing garments.

Wine-Stained Cables Hat and Scarf

Subtle, sophisticated coloring meets simple cables in this lovely hat and scarf. While the cables add knitting interest, the dye pattern remains the center of attention. And since the lofty cable pattern on the scarf is reversible, both sides look equally fabulous.

Finished Size **Hat:** 20 (21)" (51 [53.5] cm) head circumference and 7¾ (8½)" (19.5 [21.5] cm) tall. To fit a medium (large) adult. **Scarf:** 7" (18 cm) wide and 60" (152.5 cm) long.

Yarn *Worsted weight wool:* about 223 yd (204 m) white. We used Patons Classic Merino Wool (100% wool; 223 yd [204 m]/100 g): #201 winter white, 1 ball. *Sportweight brushed mohair or brushed mohair blend:* about 186 yd (170 m) off-white. We used Berroco Mohair Classic (78% mohair, 13% wool, 9% nylon; 93 yd [85 m]/43 g): #8233 off-white, 2 balls.

Needles **Hat:** Size 8 (5 mm): set of 4 double-pointed (dpn) and 16" (40-cm) circular (cir). **Scarf:** Size 13 (9 mm): straight. Adjust needle size if necessary to obtain the correct gauge.

Notions Cable needle (cn); stitch markers (m); tapestry needle.

Gauge 20 sts and 26 rnds = 4" (10 cm) in St st worked in the round on size 8 (5 mm) needles with Classic Merino

Dye-Palette Pattern Multicolor #2

black plum   slate blue   black

Dye Style: Multicolor Graduated-Band.

Dye: Rit: black plum, slate blue, and black.

Dye Recipe: Mix ¼ teaspoon (1.2 ml) black plum dye with ¼ cup (60 ml) white vinegar and 9 cups (2 liters) hot water.

Special Dyeing Instructions Add ¼ teaspoon (1.2 ml) black plum dye mixed with 2 tablespoons (30 ml) water when ⅙ of the yarn has been dyed. When ⅓ of the yarn has been dyed, discard the dyebath and mix another dyebath with ¼ teaspoon (1.2 ml) slate blue dye with ¼ cup (60 ml) white vinegar and 9 cups (2 liters) hot water. Proceed as before. When about ⅓ of the yarn is left, add ½ teaspoon (2.5 ml) black dye mixed with 2 tablespoons (30 ml) of water to the existing dyebath.

Yardage for Each Yarn Ball **Hat:** 1 ball wool yarn containing 223 yd (204 m). **Scarf:** 1 ball mohair yarn containing 186 yd (170 m).

Amount of Undyed Reserve Yarn None.

Wool; 28 sts and 14½ rows = 4" (10 cm) in cable pattern worked in rows on size 13 (9 mm) needles with Mohair Classic.

Hat

Cable band: With size 8 (5 mm) dpn or cir needle and beg at light end of the dyed wool yarn, CO 20 sts. Do not join into a rnd; instead work back and forth in rows as foll:

Row 1: [K4, p4] 2 times, k4.

Rows 2 and 4: K8, p4, k8.

Row 3: K4, p4, slip (sl) next 2 sts to cable needle (cn) and hold in front, k2, k2 from cn, p4, k4.

Row 5: Rep Row 1.

Row 6: Rep Row 2.

Rep Rows 1–6 until piece measures about 20 (21)" (51 [53.5] cm) from beg, ending with Row 6. BO all sts. With yarn threaded on a tapestry needle, sew CO and BO edges tog, matching cable patt.

Crown: With size 8 (5 mm) cir needle and RS facing, pick up and knit 70 (80) sts evenly along one selvedge edge of cable band. Join for working in the rnd and place marker (pm) to indicate beg of rnd (slip marker every rnd). Work even in St st (knit all sts every rnd) until crown measures 1½ (2)" (3.8 [5] cm) from pick-up rnd. *For the larger size only:* Work 2 rnds as foll: *K6, k2tog; rep from * around; then knit 1 rnd even—70 sts rem for both sizes. Change to dpns as necessary.

Shape top: Cont for both sizes as foll:

Rnd 1: *K5, k2tog; rep from * around—60 sts rem.

Rnds 2, 4, 6, 8, 10, 12: Knit.

Rnd 3: *K4, k2tog; rep from * around—50 sts rem.

Rnd 5: *K3, k2tog; rep from * around—40 sts rem.

Rnd 7: *K2, k2tog; rep from * around—30 sts rem.

Rnd 9: *K1, k2tog; rep from * around—20 sts rem.

Rnd 11: *K2tog; rep from * around—10 sts rem.

Rnd 13: Rep Rnd 11—5 sts rem.

Cut yarn, leaving a 12" (30.5-cm) tail. Thread tail on tapestry needle and draw through rem sts. Pull snugly to close top of hat, and fasten off on inside. Weave in ends.

Scarf

With size 13 (9 mm) straight needles and beg at light end of the dyed mohair yarn, CO 28 sts. Work 2 set-up rows as foll:

Set-up row 1: (RS) [K4, p4] 3 times, k4.

Set-up row 2: [P4, k4] 3 times, p4.

Work reversible cable patt as foll:

Row 1: (RS) *Slip (sl) 2 sts onto cable needle (cn) and hold in front, k2, k2 from cn, p4; rep from * 2 more times, sl 2 sts onto cn and hold in front, k2, k2 from cn.

Row 2: *P4, sl 2 sts onto cn and hold in front, k2, k2 from cn; rep from * 2 more times, p4. *Note:* On this row, the cable crossings are worked on the sts that weren't crossed for cables in Row 1.

Rows 3 and 5: [K4, p4] 3 times, k4.

Rows 4 and 6: [P4, k4] 3 times, p4.

Rep Rows 1–6 (do not rep set-up rows) until piece measures 60" (152.5 cm) from beg, ending with Row 6 so the last cable crossing row is 2 rows from the end. BO all sts. Weave in ends.

School's Out Summer Shell

This comfy top will brighten any little girl's playtime. The cotton yarn, wound in a tight ball, absorbs dye relatively slowly. These factors make the color bands, dyed in multiple dyebaths, more clear and pronounced.

Finished Size 25 (27, 29)" (63.5 [68.5, 73.5] cm) chest circumference. To fit child sizes 2 (6, 8) years.

Yarn Worsted-weight cotton: about 336 (420, 420) yd [308 (385, 385) m] white. We used Mission Falls 1824 Cotton (100% cotton; 84 yd [77 m]/50 g): #102 ivory, 4 (5, 5) skeins.

Needles Size 7 (4.5 mm): straight. Adjust needle size if necessary to obtain the correct gauge.

Notions Safety pin or waste yarn; stitch holder; tapestry needle.

Gauge 18 sts and 30 rows = 4" (10 cm) in basket weave patt.

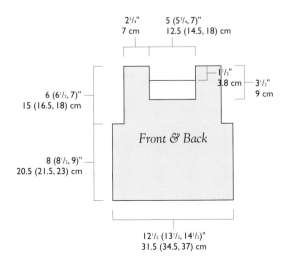

2¾"
7 cm

5 (5¾, 7)"
12.5 (14.5, 18) cm

1½"
3.8 cm — 3½"
9 cm

6 (6½, 7)"
15 (16.5, 18) cm

Front & Back

8 (8½, 9)"
20.5 (21.5, 23) cm

12½ (13½, 14½)"
31.5 (34.5, 37) cm

Dye-Pattern Palette Multicolor #3

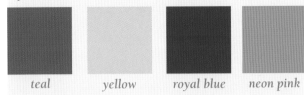

teal · yellow · royal blue · neon pink

Dye Style Multicolor Graduated-Band.

Dye Rit: teal, yellow, royal blue, and neon pink. *Note:* Use only Rit dye, or another dye specifically formulated for dyeing cotton.

Dye Recipe Mix 1 teaspoon (5 ml) teal dye with ¼ cup (60 ml) white vinegar and 12 cups (3 liters) hot water.

Special Dyeing Instructions When ⅓ of the yarn has been dyed, discard the dyebath. Immerse yarn in dyebath mixed with 1 teaspoon (5 ml) yellow dye, ¼ cup (60 ml) white vinegar, and 12 cups (3 l) hot water. When ⅔ of the yarn has been dyed, discard the dyebath. Immerse the yarn in a dyebath mixed with 1 teaspoon (5 ml) royal blue dye, ¼ cup (60 ml) white vinegar, and 12 cups (3 liters) hot water. When half of the remaining yarn has been dyed, discard the dyebath. Immerse the yarn in a dyebath mixed with ½ teaspoon (2.5 ml) neon pink dye, ¼ cup (60 ml) white vinegar, and 12 cups (3 liters) hot water.

Yardage for Each Yarn Ball Front and Back: 2 balls containing 168 (210, 210) yd (154 [192.5, 192.5] m) each. *Note:* Wind the yarn ball tighter than for most graduated-band projects and avoiding squeezing the ball as it lies in the initial dyebaths to help yarn in the center of the ball absorb less dye from initial dyebaths and more dye from subsequent dyebaths.

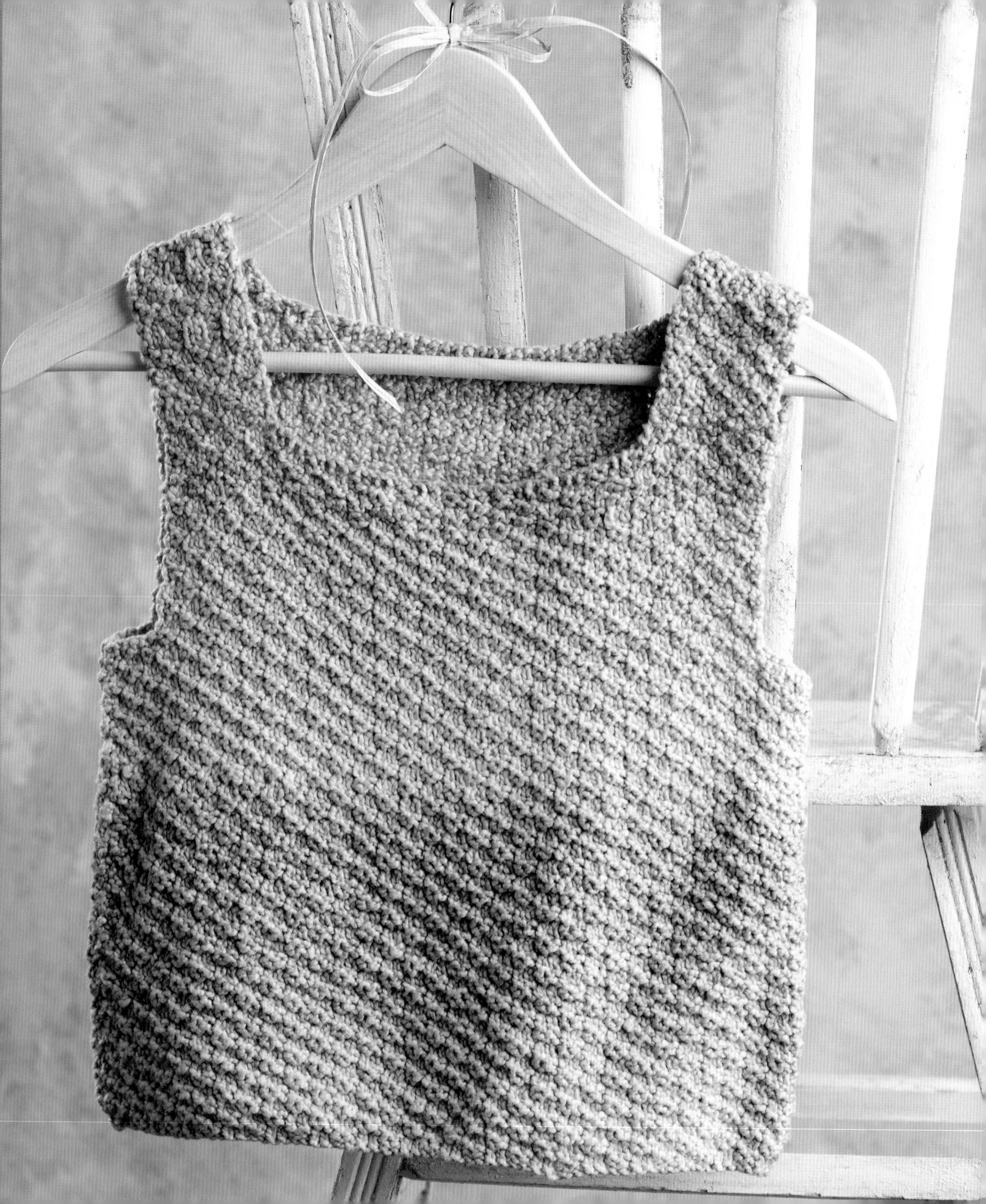

Basket Weave Pattern (*multiple of 4 sts*)

Row 1: (RS) *K2, p2; rep from * to end.

Row 2: Work all sts as they appear (knit the knit sts, and purl the purl sts).

Row 3: *P2, k2; rep from * to end.

Row 4: Rep Row 2.

Rep Rows 1–4 for patt. *Note:* Both sides of the patt look the same; to keep track of whether you are on a RS or WS row, mark the RS of the work with a piece of scrap yarn or a safety pin.

Back

Beg with pink end of yarn, CO 56 (60, 66) sts. Work in basket weave patt (see above) until piece measures 8 (8½, 9)" (20.5 [21.5, 23] cm) from beg, ending with a WS row.

Shape armholes: Cont in patt, BO 5 sts at beg of next 2 rows—46 (50, 56) sts rem. Work even in patt until armholes measure 4½ (5, 5½)" (11.5 [12.5, 14] cm), ending with a WS row.

Shape back neck: Work 12 sts in patt, BO center 22 (26, 32) sts for neck, place rem 12 sts on holder. Working back and forth on 12 shoulder sts only, work even in patt until armhole measures 6 (6½, 7)" (15 [16.5, 18] cm). BO all sts. Return 12 held sts to needle and rejoin yarn with RS facing. Work in patt until armhole measures the same as the first side. BO all sts.

Front

Work as for back until armholes measure 2½ (3, 3½)" (6.5 [7.5, 9] cm)—46 (50, 56) sts.

Shape front neck: Work as for back neck. *Note:* To make the color changes on the front match the back at the shoulders, cut the yarn on the front a few rows before beginning the front neck shaping. Discard the next several yards of yarn until you reach a place where the yarn shade matches that of the back at the same height above the armholes. Rejoin the yarn at the new place and continue working the front.

Finishing: With yarn threaded on a tapestry needle, sew front and back together along shoulders and sides. Weave in ends.

Which stitch patterns show off graduated-color-band yarns?

Garter stitch

Stockinette stitch

Reverse stockinette stitch

Allover ribbing

Allover texture (like seed stitch)

Ripple stitches (like feather-and-fan)

Cable patterns

school's out summer shell

Chapter 5

Zigzag Projects

Zigzag yarns are the wild children of the self-patterning bunch. Sometimes their pattern repeats are easily distinguished; sometimes you have to squint to see them. When you look closely, you see that the patterns created by zigzag yarns are more than simple variegation; the repeats show a mathematical precision. Streaks and splotches appear as you knit, delightfully surprising every time. And the colors in these streaks and splotches are what grabs everyone's attention. Check out the projects in this chapter for ideas, and remember to experiment!

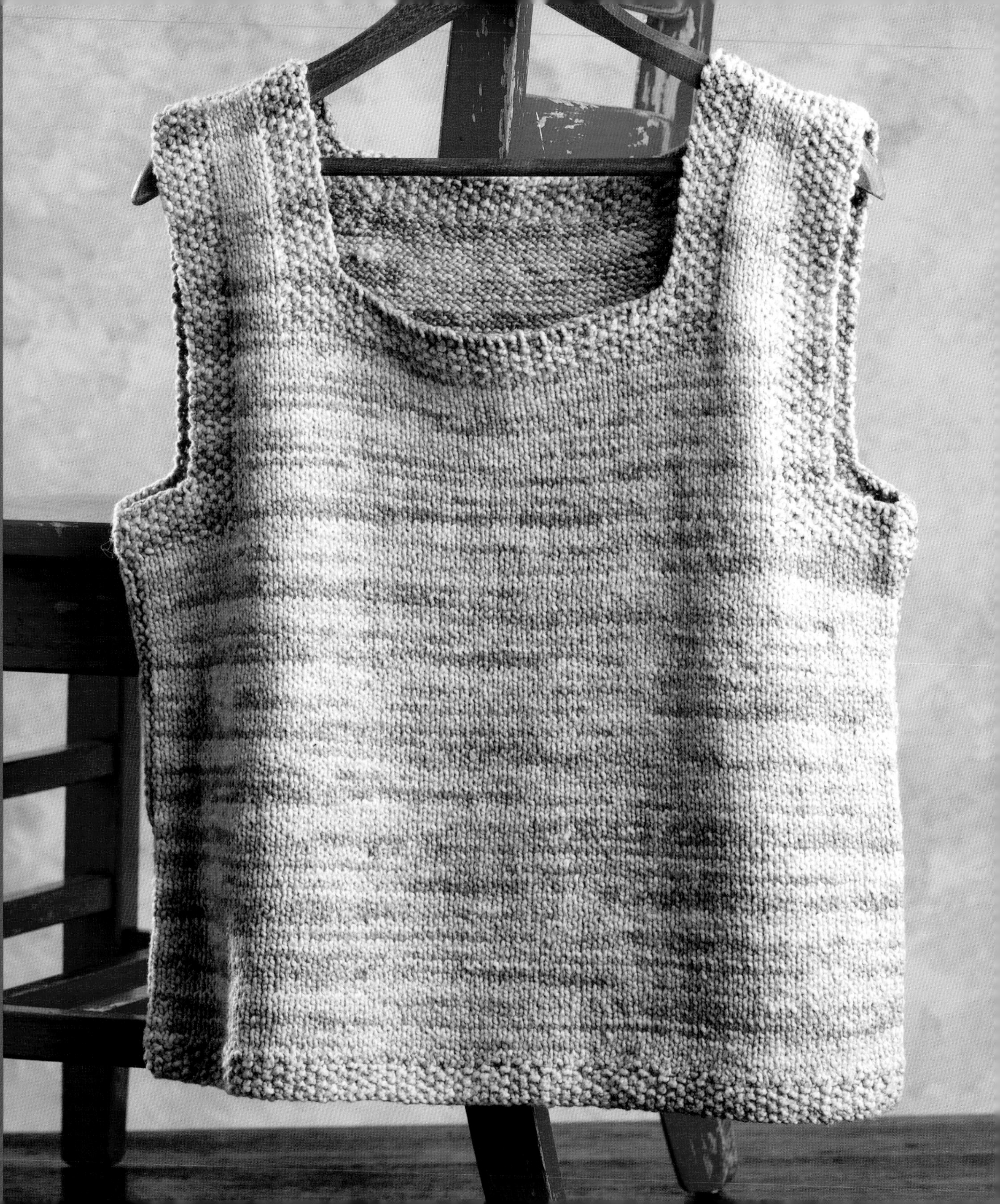

Cool Blues Summer Shell

Keep cool in this sleeveless cotton top. The zigzag pattern is forgiving of changes to the number of live stitches at neck and armholes, and the shell knits up in a snap.

Finished Size 37 (39, 41, 43)" (94 [99, 104, 109] cm) chest/bust circumference. To fit adult women's small (medium, large, extra-large).

Yarn *Worsted-weight cotton:* about 588 (672, 756, 840) yd [539 (616, 693, 770) m] off-white. We used Mission Falls 1824 Cotton (100% cotton; 84 yd [77 m]/50 g): #102 ivory, 7 (8, 9, 10) balls.

Needles Size 7 (4.5 mm): straight. Adjust needle size if necessary to obtain the correct gauge.

Notions Stitch markers (m; optional); tapestry needle.

Gauge 18 sts and 28 rows = 4" (10 cm) in St st.

Seed Stitch

Row 1: *K1, p1; rep from * to end, working last st as k1 if there is an odd number of sts.
Row 2: Knit the purl sts and purl the knit sts.
Rep Row 2 for patt.

Note: You may begin with either end of the yarn. Remember to unwrap all the skeins in the same direction when you're winding them into balls for knitting; doing so makes

Dye-Pattern Palette Zigzag #1

evening blue   periwinkle

Dye Style Zigzag.

Dyes Rit: periwinkle and evening blue.

Dye Recipes Mix ½ teaspoon (2.5 ml) periwinkle dye with 2 tablespoons (30 ml) white vinegar and 1 cup (240 ml) hot water. Mix 1 teaspoon (5 ml) evening blue dye with 2 tablespoons (30 ml) white vinegar and 1 cup (240 ml) hot water.

Skein Length 40 feet (12 m).

Special Dyeing Instructions Wind several manageable-sized skeins to avoid having to saturate all of the yarn strands in one big skein.

Dye Pattern Lengths 90" (229 cm) periwinkle; 36" (91.5 cm) evening blue; 36" (91.5 cm) periwinkle; 72" (183 cm) evening blue; 72" (183 cm) periwinkle; 90" (229 cm) evening blue; 36" (91.5 cm) periwinkle; remainder evening blue.

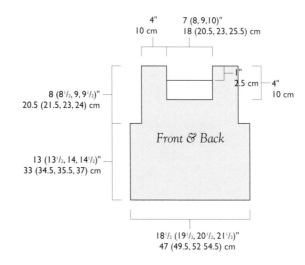

4"
10 cm
7 (8, 9, 10)"
18 (20.5, 23, 25.5) cm
1"
2.5 cm
4"
10 cm
8 (8½, 9, 9½)"
20.5 (21.5, 23, 24) cm
13 (13½, 14, 14½)"
33 (34.5, 35.5, 37) cm
Front & Back
18½ (19½, 20½, 21½)"
47 (49.5, 52 54.5) cm

it easy to resume at the same point in the color sequence when you join a new ball in the middle of a piece.

Back

CO 83 (88, 92, 97) sts. Work in seed st (see above) for 6 rows. Change to St st (knit all sts on RS, purl all sts on WS), and work even until piece measures 12 (12½, 13, 13½)" (30.5 [31.5, 33, 34.5] cm) from beg, ending with a WS row. *Armhole borders:* (RS) Establish seed st borders at each side as foll: Work 14 sts in seed st, work center 55 (60, 64, 69) sts in St st, work rem 14 sts in seed st. (You may want to use stitch markers to denote the boundaries between the seed-st and St st sections.) Work 5 more rows as established, ending with a WS row—piece should measure about 13 (13½, 14, 14½)" (33 [34.5, 35.5, 37] cm) from beg.

Shape armholes: (RS) BO 8 sts, work in seed st until there are 6 sts on the right needle, knit to last 14 sts, work in seed st to end—75 (80, 84, 89) sts rem. *Next row:* (WS)

BO 8 sts, work in seed st until there are 6 sts on right needle, purl to last 6 sts, work in seed st to end—67 (72, 76, 81) sts rem. Keeping the first 6 and last 6 sts in seed st as established, work even until armholes measure 6 (6½, 7, 7½)" (15 [16.5, 18, 19] cm), ending with a WS row.

Back neck border: (RS) Work first 6 sts in seed st, k6, work center 43 (48, 52, 57) sts in seed st, k6, work last 6 sts in seed st. *Next row:* (WS) Work first 6 sts in seed st, p6, work center 43 (48, 52, 57) sts in seed st, p6, work last 6 sts in seed st. Rep the last 2 rows 2 more times, ending with a WS row—6 seed st rows completed at center; armholes should measure about 7 (7½, 8, 8½)" (18 [19, 20.5, 21.5] cm).

Shape back neck: (RS) Work first 6 sts in seed st, k6, work 6 sts in seed st, join second ball of yarn and BO center 31 (36, 40, 45) sts, work 6 sts in seed st, k6, work 6 sts in seed st—18 sts at each side. Working each side separately, cont in patts as established with 6 sts at each side of each shoulder in seed st. Work even until armholes measure 8 (8½, 9, 9½)" (20.5 [21.5, 23, 24] cm. BO all sts.

Front

Work as for back until armholes measure 3 (3½, 4, 4½)" (7.5 [9, 10, 11.5] cm), ending with a WS row—67 (72, 76, 81) sts.

Front neck border: Work 6 rows as for back neck border—armholes should measure about 4 (4½, 5, 5½)" (10 [11.5, 12.5, 14] cm).

Shape front neck: Work as for back neck.

Finishing

With yarn threaded on a tapestry needle, sew front and back together along shoulder and side seams. Weave in ends.

Garden Colors Pillow Tops

Self-patterning yarns aren't just for apparel; they're great for home décor, too. These square pillow tops are simple to knit, and they make great canvases for displaying your dyeing.

Finished Size About 12" (30.5-cm) square.

Yarn *Unplied worsted-weight wool:* about 119 yd (110 m) white for each pillow top. We used Alafoss Lopi (100% Icelandic wool; 119 yd [110 m]/100 g): #51 white, 1 skein per pillow top. Yarn distributed by JCA/Reynolds Yarns.

Needles Pillow: Size 10½ (6.5 mm), straight. **I-cord edging** (optional): Size 10½ (6.5 mm): 2 double-pointed (dpn). Adjust needle size if necessary to obtain the correct gauge.

Notions Tapestry needle; size G (4.5 mm) crochet hook; one 14" (35.5-cm) square sturdy coordinated backing fabric for each pillow; polyester fiberfill for stuffing; sharp-pointed sewing needle and matching sewing thread for assembling pillows; embellishments (beads, buttons, cording) as desired.

Gauge 13 sts and 15 rows = 4" (10 cm) in St st.

Dye-Pattern Palette Zigzag #2

avocado   apricot   ripe tomato   chestnut

Dye Style Zigzag.

Dyes Country Classics: avocado, chestnut, apricot, and ripe tomato.

Dye Recipes For each of the avocado, chestnut, and apricot dyes, mix ½ teaspoon (2.5 ml) dye with 2 tablespoons (30 ml) white vinegar and 1 cup (240 ml) hot water. Mix ¼ teaspoon (1.2 ml) avocado dye with 2 tablespoons (30 ml) white vinegar and 1 cup (240 ml) hot water (to make light avocado). Mix 2 teaspoons (10 ml) ripe tomato dye with 2 tablespoons (30 ml) white vinegar and 1 cup (240 ml) hot water.

Skein Length 40 feet (12 m).

Dye Pattern Lengths 36" (91.5 cm) light avocado; 36" (91.5 cm) avocado; 16" (40.5 cm) ripe tomato; 24" (61 cm) avocado; 6" (15 cm) light avocado; 4" (10 cm) apricot; 6" (15 cm) avocado; 3" (7.5 cm) chestnut; 6" (15 cm) avocado; 3" (7.5 cm) ripe tomato; 28" (71 cm) light avocado; 72" (183 cm) avocado; 8" (20.5 cm) chestnut; 24" (61 cm) apricot; 90" (229 cm) light avocado; 8" (20.5 cm) chestnut; remainder avocado.

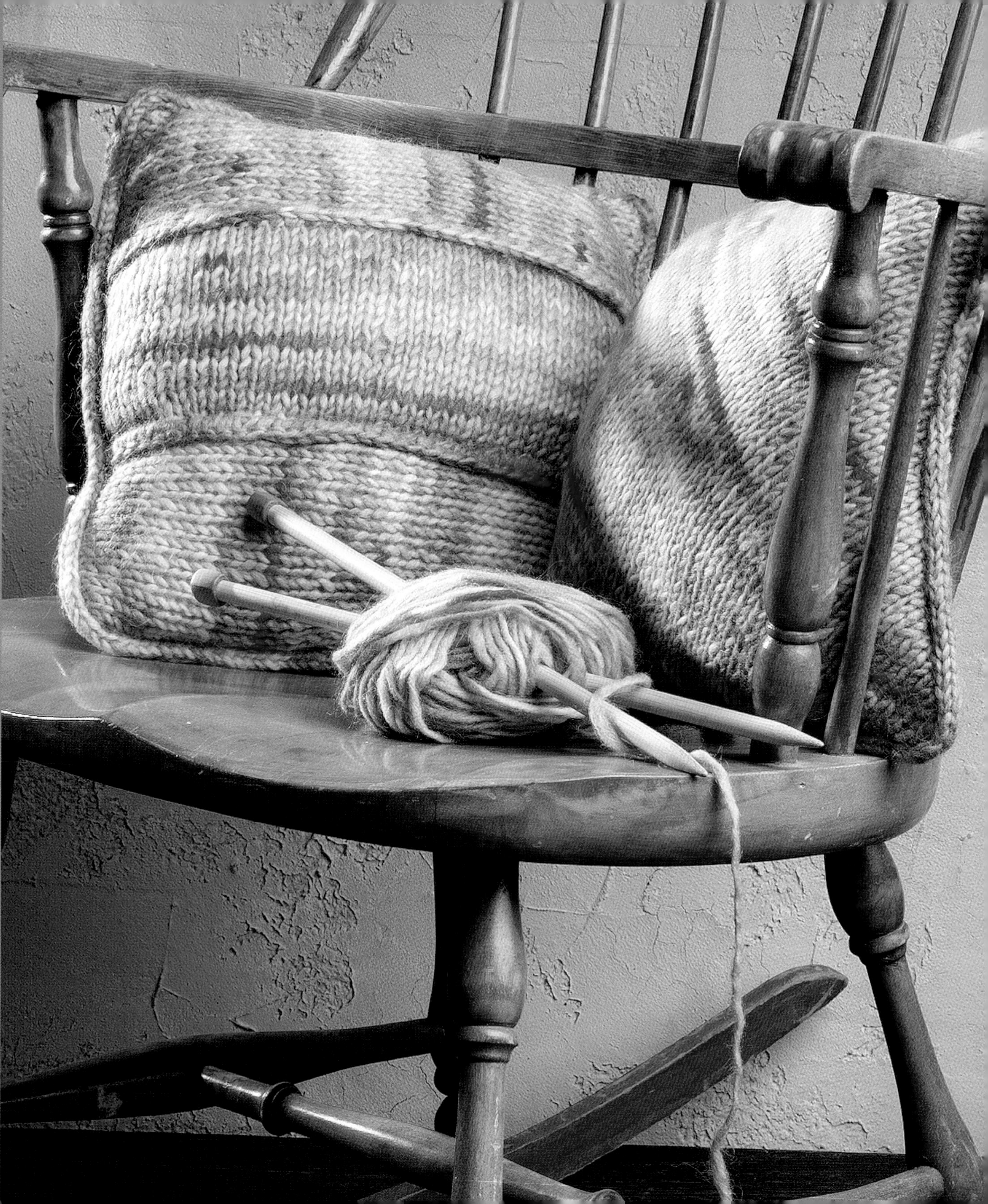

Pillow Top #1

CO 40 sts. Work even in St st (knit all sts on RS; purl all sts on WS) until piece measures 12½" (31.5 cm) from beg. BO all sts. Weave in ends. Either side of the fabric can be designated the "public" side.

Pillow Top #2

CO 3 sts. Knit 1 row.

Row 1: (RS) Using the backward loop method (see Glossary, page 99), CO 1 st, knit to end, pick up and knit 1 st from base of last st—2 sts inc'd.

Row 2: CO 1 st as before, purl to end, pick up and purl 1 st from base of last st—2 sts inc'd.

Rep the last 2 rows 15 more times, ending with Row 2—67 sts; piece should measure about 8¾" (22 cm) straight up the center from the initial CO, and about 12½" (31.5 cm) along one side. Dec as foll:

Row 1: (RS) K2tog, knit to last 2 sts, k2tog—2 sts dec'd.

Row 2: P2tog, purl to last 2 sts, p2tog—2 sts dec'd.

Rep the last 2 rows 15 more times, ending with Row 2—3 sts rem. K3tog—1 st rem. Cut yarn and draw tail through last st to fasten off. Weave in ends.

Pillow Top #3

Vertical side pieces: (make 2) CO 14 sts. Work even in St st until piece measures 13" (33 cm) from beg. BO all sts.

Horizontal center piece: CO 42 sts. Work even in St st until piece measures 4¾" (12 cm) from beg. BO all sts.

Assembly: Hold the selvedge of one vertical side piece tog with the CO edge of center piece so that WS of pieces are touching. With RS facing and using a crochet hook, work single crochet (sc; see Glossary, page 100) to join pieces together. Cut yarn and fasten off. Hold selvedge of rem vertical piece tog with BO edge of center piece, and join with sc in the same manner. Weave in ends.

Finishing

Wash and block each pillow top so it's square. Using the pillow top as template, cut a matching piece of backing fabric. With RS of pillow top and backing held tog, use sewing needle and matching thread to sew around all sides, using a ¼" (0.6 cm) seam allowance and leaving a 6" (15-cm) opening along one edge. Trim the woven fabric (not the knitted fabric) corners, turn the pillow top right side out through the opening, and stuff firmly with polyester fiberfill. Fold in the raw edges of the opening and sew the opening closed.

I-cord edging: (optional) With dpn, CO 3 sts. Work I-cord (see Glossary, page 99) long enough to fit around all four sides of the pillow. Cut yarn, leaving a 2-foot (61-cm) tail. Place rem sts on a piece of scrap yarn. With yarn threaded on a tapestry needle and beg at one pillow corner with CO end of I-cord, sew I-cord edging in place to the knitted pillow top, stopping about 3"–4" (7.5–10 cm) from the corner where you began. Adjust the length of the I-cord to fit exactly, either by working more rows or unraveling rows. Finish attaching I-cord, and sew 3 live sts of I-cord to bases of 3 CO sts. Weave in ends. Add beads, buttons, cording, or other embellishments if desired.

Which stitch patterns show off zigzag yarns?
Garter stitch
Stockinette stitch
Reverse stockinette stitch
All-over texture (such as seed stitch)

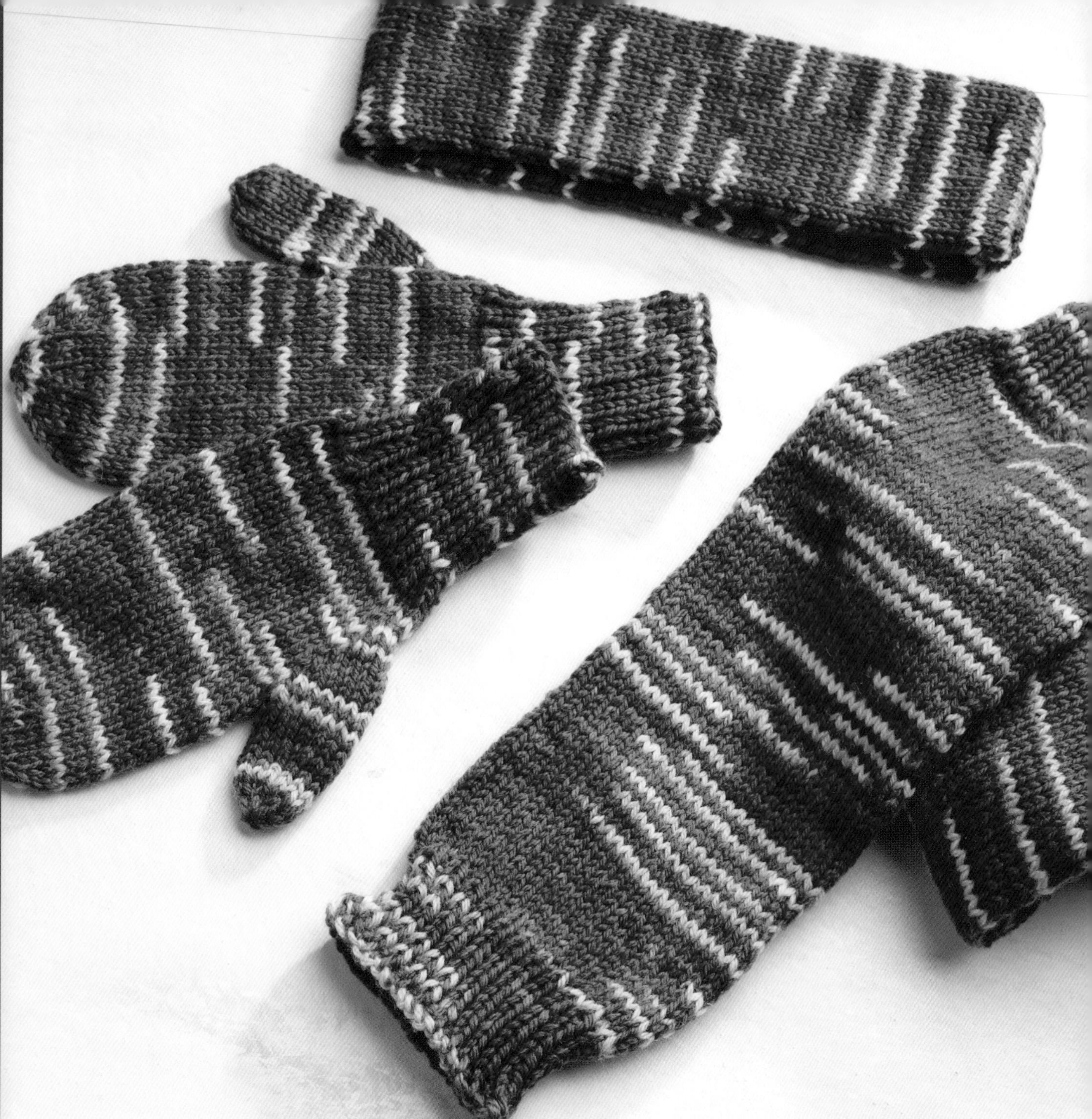

Harbor Lights
Leg Warmer Set

These mittens and headband are worked according to the same easy pattern as those in the Autumn Sparkle set (page 39), but what a difference the change of yarns makes! In these pieces, streaks of bright color shine against a dark, handpainted blue background.

Finished Size **Mittens:** 7 (8)" (18 [20.5] cm) hand circumference and 9¾ (11)" (25 [28] cm) long from base of cuff to tip. **Headband:** 20 (21)" (51 [53.5] cm) head circumference and 3" (7.5 cm) wide. ***Leg warmers:*** 10 (11)" (25.5 [28] cm) upper leg circumference and 13½ (14½)" (34.5 [37] cm) long. Mittens to fit women's small/medium (women's large/men's small); headband and leg warmers to fit adult small/medium (medium/large).

Yarn Worsted-weight wool: about 446 (669) yd [408 (612) m] white. We used Patons Classic Merino Wool (100% wool; 223 yd [204 m]/100 g): #201 winter white, 2 (3) balls.

Needles Size 8 (5 mm): set of 4 double-pointed (dpn). Adjust needle size if necessary to obtain the correct gauge.

Notions Stitch markers (m); tapestry needle; 2 safety pins or 1 stitch holder.

Gauge 20½ sts and 28 rnds = 4" (10 cm) in St st worked in the round.

Mittens

Work as for Autumn Sparkle Mittens on page 39.

Headband

CO 30 sts. Work as for Autumn Sparkle Headband on page 39.

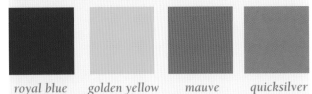

Dye-Pattern Palette Zigzag #3

royal blue	golden yellow	mauve	quicksilver

Dye Style Zigzag.

Dyes Rit: royal blue, golden yellow, and mauve; Country Classics: quicksilver.

Dye Recipe For each of the royal blue, golden yellow, mauve, and quicksilver dyes, mix ½ teaspoon (2.5 ml) of dye with 2 tablespoons (30 ml) white vinegar and 1 cup (240 ml) hot water.

Skein Length 40 feet (12 m).

Dye Pattern Lengths 8" (20.5 cm) golden yellow; 44" (112 cm) royal blue; 8" (20.5 cm) quicksilver; 72" (183 cm) royal blue; 8" (20.5 cm) mauve; 90" (229 cm) royal blue; 8" (20.5 cm) mauve; 44" (112 cm) royal blue; 8" (20.5 cm) quicksilver; remainder royal blue.

Leg Warmers *(make 2)*

Note: Leg warmers are knitted from the top down. CO 52 (56) sts. Divide sts as evenly as possible on 3 dpn. Join for working in the rnd and place marker (pm) to indicate beg of rnd (slip marker every rnd). *Next rnd:* *K1, p1; rep from * around. Rep this rnd 11 more times—12 rnds of ribbing completed; piece should measure about 1¾" (4.5 cm) from beg. Change to St st (knit all sts every rnd) and work even until piece measures 6" (15 cm) from beg. *Dec Rnd 1:* *K11 (12), k2tog; rep from * around—48 (52) sts rem. Work even for 2" (5 cm). *Dec Rnd 2:* *K10 (11), k2tog; rep from * around—44 (48) sts rem. Work even for 3¾ (4¾)" (9.5 [12] cm), or until piece measures 1¾" (4.5 cm) less than desired total length. *Dec Rnd 3:* Knit, dec 2 sts evenly spaced—42 (46) sts rem. *Next rnd:* *K1, p1; rep from * around. Rep this rnd 11 more times—12 rnds of ribbing completed; piece should measure about 13½ (14½)" (34.5 [37] cm) from beg. BO all sts loosely in rib patt. Weave in ends.

Chapter 6

Striping Projects

If zigzag yarns are the wild children of the self-patterning bunch, then we may think of striping yarns as the lovely but conventional kids. Striping yarns imitate the stripes knitted into more traditional projects, in which one yarn is changed for another at the beginning of a row or round. The fun of knitting with self-striping yarns would seem to be mostly in the tidiness of process; you needn't weave in ends. However, if you let your imagination go, striping yarns can still produce surprising results!

Child's Watermelon Sweater and Socks

Add a taste of summer to any season with this clever set! The seeds are dotted on with a black fabric pen, and they can be added after the sweater and socks are knitted up to ensure aesthetically pleasing placement.

Finished Size Sweater: 23 (25)" (58.5 [63.5] cm) chest circumference. Socks: About 5" (12.5 cm) foot circumference and 4½ (5½)" (11.5 [14] cm) long from heel to toe. To fit child's size 2 (4) years.

Yarn *Sportweight wool:* about 552 (736) yd [504 (672) m] off-white. We used Brown Sheep Nature Spun Sport (100% wool; 184 yd [168 m]/50 g): #730 natural, 3 (4) balls.

Needles Sweater ribbing: Size 5 (3.75 mm) straight and 16" (40-cm) circular (cir). **Sweater body and sleeves:** Size 6 (4 mm) straight. **Socks:** Size 3 (3.25 mm) set of 4 double-pointed (dpn). Adjust needle size if necessary to obtain the correct gauge.

Notions Contrasting waste yarn; stitch marker (m); stitch holder; tapestry needle; black fabric pen (we used Painters Medium Fabric Pen, by the Hunt Corporation).

Gauge Sweater: 22½ sts and 30 rows = 4" (10 cm) in St st worked in rows on size 6 (4 mm) needles. **Socks**: 29 sts and 40 rnds = 4" (10 cm) in St st worked in the round on size 3 (3.25 mm) needles.

Dye-Pattern Palette Stripe #1

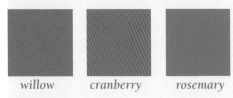

willow   cranberry   rosemary

Dye Style Stripe.

Dyes Gaywool Bush Blend Colors: willow, rosemary, and cranberry.

Dye Recipes For each of the willow, rosemary, and cranberry dyes, mix ½ teaspoon (2.5 ml) dye with 2 tablespoons (30 ml) white vinegar and 1 cup (240 ml) hot water.

Skein Length 40 feet (12 m).

Special Dyeing Instructions Wind 1 skein with 78 yd (71 m) of yarn for the socks (all sizes). Wind the rest of the yarn—474 (658) yd (433 [601] m)—into a single skein for the sweater.

Dye Pattern Lengths for Sweater Divide the skein into quarters and mark the divisions by tying contrasting yarn at the measurements. Paint 1 section with cranberry dye. Dilute the remaining cranberry dye with an equal amount of water and paint the next section with diluted cranberry to make the color increasingly lighter up to the next division marker. Leave the next section undyed. Divide the final section in half. Paint the first half with rosemary. Paint the last half with willow.

Dye Pattern Lengths for Socks Paint as for the sweater yarn except that the undyed section should only be 36" (91.5 cm) long; paint the remainder of that section with rosemary.

Adding the Seeds After the yarn has been dyed, heat-set, rinsed, and dried, draw seeds on the yarn while it is still in the skein by using black fabric pen. Dot seeds at 2" (5-cm) intervals for 36" (91.5 cm) at the division between the light and dark cranberry colors. If you prefer, you may wait until the sweater and socks are knitted, then add the seeds to the knitted fabric. Heat-set the seeds, if necessary, according to the fabric pen instructions.

Sweater

Back

With size 5 (3.75 mm) straight needles and sweater yarn, CO 64 (70) sts. *Next row:* *K1, p1; rep from * to end. Rep this row 8 more times—9 rows of ribbing completed; piece should measure about 1" (2.5 cm) from beg. Change to size 6 (4 mm) needles and work in St st (knit all sts on RS, purl all sts on WS) until piece measures 11 (12)" (28 [30.5] cm) from beg, ending with a WS row.

Shape shoulders: Cont in St st, BO 18 sts at the beg of the next 2 rows—28 (34) sts rem. On the next row, BO rem sts.

Front

Note: Wind off a small ball of sweater yarn that contains at least one full repeat of the color pattern and set it aside to use for one side of the front neck. Work as for back until piece measures 9 (10)" (23 [25.5] cm) from beg, ending with a WS row—64 (70) sts.

Shape front neck: K27, place center 10 (16) sts on holder, join the small ball of yarn at the same place in the color repeat as the working yarn for the first side of the neck, knit to end—27 sts at each side. Working each side separately, dec 1 st at each neck edge every row 9 times—18 sts rem at each side. Cont even until front measures 11 (12)" (28 [30.5] cm) from beg. BO all sts.

Sleeves

With size 5 (3.75 mm) straight needles and sweater yarn, CO 36 (40) sts. *Next row:* *K1, p1; rep from * to end. Rep this row 11 more times—12 rows of ribbing completed; piece should measure about 1½" (3.8 cm) from beg. Change to size 6 (4 mm) needles and work in St

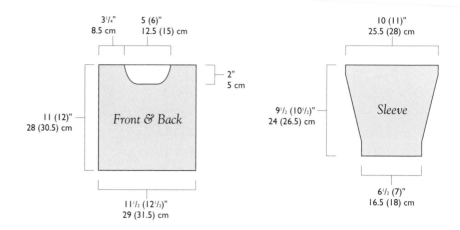

st, inc 1 st at each end of needle every 4th row 10 (11) times—56 (62) sts. Work even until piece measures 9½ (10½)" (24 [26.5] cm) from beg. BO all sts.

Finishing

With yarn threaded on a tapestry needle, sew front and back tog at shoulders.

Neckband: With size 5 (3.75 mm) cir needle, sweater yarn, RS facing, and beg at left shoulder seam, pick up and knit 12 (14) sts along left side of front neck, k10 (16) sts from holder at center front, and pick up and knit 12 (14) sts along right side of front neck and 30 (34) sts across back neck—64 (78) sts total. Join for working in the rnd and place marker to indicate beg of rnd (slip marker every rnd). *Next rnd:* *K1, p1; rep from * around. Rep this rnd 7 more times—8 rnds ribbing completed. BO all sts loosely in patt.

With yarn threaded on tapestry needle, sew sleeves into armholes, aligning the center of each sleeve top with the shoulder seam. Sew sleeve and side seams. Weave in ends. If you haven't done so already, use the black fabric pen to draw the "seeds" on the cranberry-colored portions.

Socks

Note: The same number of stitches is used for both sizes; the foot length differs.

Leg: With size 3 (3.25 mm) dpn and sock yarn, CO 36 sts. Divide sts evenly on 3 dpn. Join for working in the rnd and place marker to indicate beg of rnd (slip marker every rnd). *Next rnd:* *K1, p1; rep from * around. Rep this rnd 14 more times—15 rnds of ribbing completed, piece should measure about 1½" (3.8 cm) from beg. Work even in St st (knit all sts every rnd) until piece measure 3½" (9 cm) from beg.

Heel: Arrange sts so that there are 18 sts each on 2 dpn. The dpn with the working yarn attached is the heel needle; the other dpn holds sts for the instep (to be worked later). Work the 18 heel sts in short-rows as foll:

Short-row 1: Turn and work across sts on WS as foll: Slip (sl) 1, purl to last st on heel needle, leave last st unworked, turn.

Short-row 2: (RS) Sl 1, knit to last st on needle, leave last st unworked, turn.

Short-row 3: Sl 1, purl to last 2 sts, leave last 2 sts unworked, turn.

Short-row 4: Sl 1, knit to last 2 sts, leave last 2 sts unworked, turn.

Cont in this manner, leaving 1 more st unworked at the end of the needle every row before turning, until there are 5 unworked sts at each end of needle (there will be 8 sts in the center), ending with a RS (knit) row.

Turning-row 1: (WS) Sl 1, p7, sl next st, lift strand between the needles onto left needle by inserting left needle tip under the strand from back to front, return slipped st to left needle, p2tog (slipped st and lifted strand), turn.

Turning-row 2: Sl 1, k8, sl next st, M1 (see Glossary, page 100), pass slipped st over (psso), turn.

Turning-row 3: Sl 1, p9, sl next st, lift strand between needles onto left needle as in Turning-row 1, return slipped st to left needle, p2tog (slipped st and lifted strand), turn.

Turning-row 4: Sl 1, k10, sl next st, M1, psso, turn.

Cont in this manner, working 1 more st every row before slipping next st, until all of the sts have been worked—18 sts on heel needle.

Foot: Divide sts evenly on 3 dpn. Work even in St st on all sts until piece measures 3½ (4½)" (9 [11.5] cm) from center back heel, or about 1" (2.5 cm) less than desired total length.

Toe: Dec as foll:

Rnd 1: *K4, k2tog; rep from * around—30 sts rem.

Rnds 2, 4, 6, and 8: Knit.

Rnd 3: *K3, k2tog; rep from * around—24 sts rem.

Rnd 5: *K2, k2tog; rep from * around—18 sts rem.

Rnd 7: *K1, k2tog; rep from * around—12 sts rem.

Rnd 9: *K2tog; rep from * around—6 sts rem.

Cut yarn, leaving a 12" (30.5-cm) tail. Thread tail on tapestry needle and draw through rem sts. Pull snugly to close sock toe, and fasten off on inside. Weave in ends. If you haven't done so already, use the black fabric pen to draw the "seeds" on the cranberry-colored portions.

Ladies' Water-melon Socks

Why should kids have all the fun? Knit a pair of socks for yourself, too! Ours are sized for women's feet, but the dye pattern is forgiving enough to accommodate socks knitted in most sizes—just so long as there are few enough stitches per round that the stripes remain distinct.

Finished Size 7½ (7½, 8)" (19 [19, 20.5] cm) foot circumference and 8¾ (9¼, 9¾)" (22 [23.5, 25] cm) long from back of heel to toe. To fit adult women's small (medium, large)—about US shoe sizes 6 (7–8, 9–10).

Yarn *Sock- or fingering-weight yarn* (wool or wool/nylon blend): about 450 yd (410 m) off-white (all sizes). We used stash yarn.

Needles Size 2 (2.75 mm): Set of 4 double-pointed (dpn). Adjust needle size if necessary to obtain the correct gauge.

Notions Stitch marker (m); tapestry needle.
Gauge 30 sts and 40 rnds = 4" (10 cm) in St st worked in the round.

Leg

CO 56 (56, 60) sts. Divide sts on 3 dpn as foll: 18 (18, 20) sts on the first needle, 20 (20, 20) sts on the second needle, and 18 (18, 20) sts on the third needle. Join for working in the rnd and place marker to indicate beg of rnd (slip marker every rnd). *Next rnd:* *K1, p1; rep from * around. Rep this rnd 14 more times—15 rnds of ribbing completed; piece should measure about 1¼" (3.2 cm) from beg. Work even in St st (knit all sts every rnd) until piece measures about 6 (6, 6½)" (15 [15, 16.5] cm) from beg.

Heel

Arrange sts so that there are 28 (28, 30) sts each on 2 dpn. The dpn with the working yarn attached is the heel needle; the other dpn holds sts for the instep (to be worked later). Work the 28 (28, 30) heel sts in short-rows as foll:

Short-row 1: Turn and work across sts on WS as foll: Slip (sl) 1, purl to last st on heel needle, leave last st unworked, turn.

Short-row 2: (RS) Sl 1, knit to last st, leave last st unworked, turn.

Short-row 3: Sl 1, purl to last 2 sts, leave last 2 sts unworked, turn.

Short-row 4: Sl 1, knit to last 2 sts, leave last 2 sts unworked, turn.

Cont in this manner, leaving 1 more st unworked at the end of the needle every row before turning, until there are 10 (10, 11) unworked sts at each end of needle (there with be 8 sts in the center), ending with a RS (knit) row.

Turning-row 1: (WS) Sl 1, p7, sl next st, lift strand between the needles onto left needle by inserting left needle tip under the strand from back to front, return slipped st to left needle, p2tog (slipped st and lifted strand), turn.

Turning-row 2: Sl 1, k8, sl next st, M1 (see Glossary, page 100), pass slipped st over (psso), turn.

Turning-row 3: Sl 1, p9, sl next st, lift strand between needles onto left needle as in Turning-row 1, return slipped st to left needle, p2tog (slipped st and lifted strand), turn.

Turning-row 4: Sl 1, k10, sl next st, M1, psso, turn. Cont in this manner, working 1 more st every row before slipping next st, until all of the sts have been worked—18 sts on heel needle. Cont in this manner, working 1 more

willow   cranberry   rosemary

Follow dyeing instructions for Child's Watermelon Sweater (see page 61).

st every row before increasing, until all the sts have been worked—28 (28, 30) heel sts. Divide sts on 3 dpn so that there are 18 (18, 20) sts on one needle, 18 (18, 20) sts on the second needle, and 20 (20, 20) sts on the third needle.

Foot

Work even in St st until piece measures about 7¼ (7¾, 8¼)" (18.5 [19.5, 21] cm) from center back heel (to the top of the little toe), or about 1½" (3.2 cm) less than desired total length.

Toe

For the two smallest sizes: Knit 1 rnd, working k2tog at each end of the second needle—2 sts dec'd; 54 sts rem; 18 sts on each needle. *For the largest size:* *K8, k2tog; rep from * around—54 sts rem. Cont for all sizes as foll:

Rnds 1, 3, 5, 7, 9, 11, and 13: Knit.

Rnd 2: *K7, k2tog; rep from * around—48 sts rem.

Rnd 4: *K6, k2tog; rep from * around—42 sts rem.

Rnd 6: *K5, k2tog; rep from * around—36 sts rem.

Rnd 8: *K4, k2tog; rep from * around—30 sts rem.

Rnd 10: *K3, k2tog; rep from * around—24 sts rem.

Rnd 12: *K2, k2tog; rep from * around—18 sts rem.

Rnd 14: *K1, k2tog; rep from * around—12 sts rem.

Cut yarn, leaving a 12" (30.5-cm) tail. Thread tail on tapestry needle and draw through the rem sts. Pull snugly to close sock toe, and fasten off on inside. Weave in ends.

Autumn Stripes Socks

Both these socks and the Spring Stripes Socks that follow are knitted up following the pattern for the Ladies' Watermelon Socks (page 64).

Finished Size 7½ (7½, 8)" (19 [19, 20.5] cm) foot circumference and 8¾ (9¼, 9¾)" (22 [23.5, 25] cm) long from back of heel to toe. To fit adult women's small (medium, large); about US shoe sizes 6 (7–8, 9–10).

Yarn *Sock- or fingering-weight wool or wool/nylon blend:* about 450 yd (410 m) gold (all sizes). We used stash yarn.

Needles Size 2 (2.75 mm): set of four double-pointed (dpn). Adjust needle size if necessary to obtain the correct gauge.

Notions Stitch marker (m); tapestry needle.

Gauge 30 sts and 40 rnds = 4" (10 cm) in St st worked in the round.

Socks: Work as for Adult Watermelon Socks on page 64.

Graduated-color-band, stripe, and Fair Isle self-patterning yarns are particularly suitable for adult sock patterns.

black   kelly green   chestnut   dark green

tangerine

Dye Style Stripe.

Dyes Rit: black, tangerine, dark green, kelly green. Country Classics: chestnut.

Dye Recipe For each of the black, tangerine, dark green, kelly green, and chestnut dyes, mix ½ teaspoon (2.5 ml) dye with 2 tablespoons (30 ml) white vinegar and 1 cup (240 ml) hot water.

Skein Length 40 feet (12 m).

Dye Pattern Lengths 72" (183 cm) black; 72" (183 cm) tangerine; 72" (183 cm) dark green; 72" (183 cm) tangerine; 72" (183 cm) kelly green; 72" (183 cm) chestnut; remainder undyed.

How do I knit a matching pair with self-patterning yarns?
Begin at a point where the colors change in the pattern repeat. When you cast on for the mate, find the same spot in the pattern repeat, tie the initial slip-knot for the cast-on, and proceed. Your pair will match.

autumn stripes socks

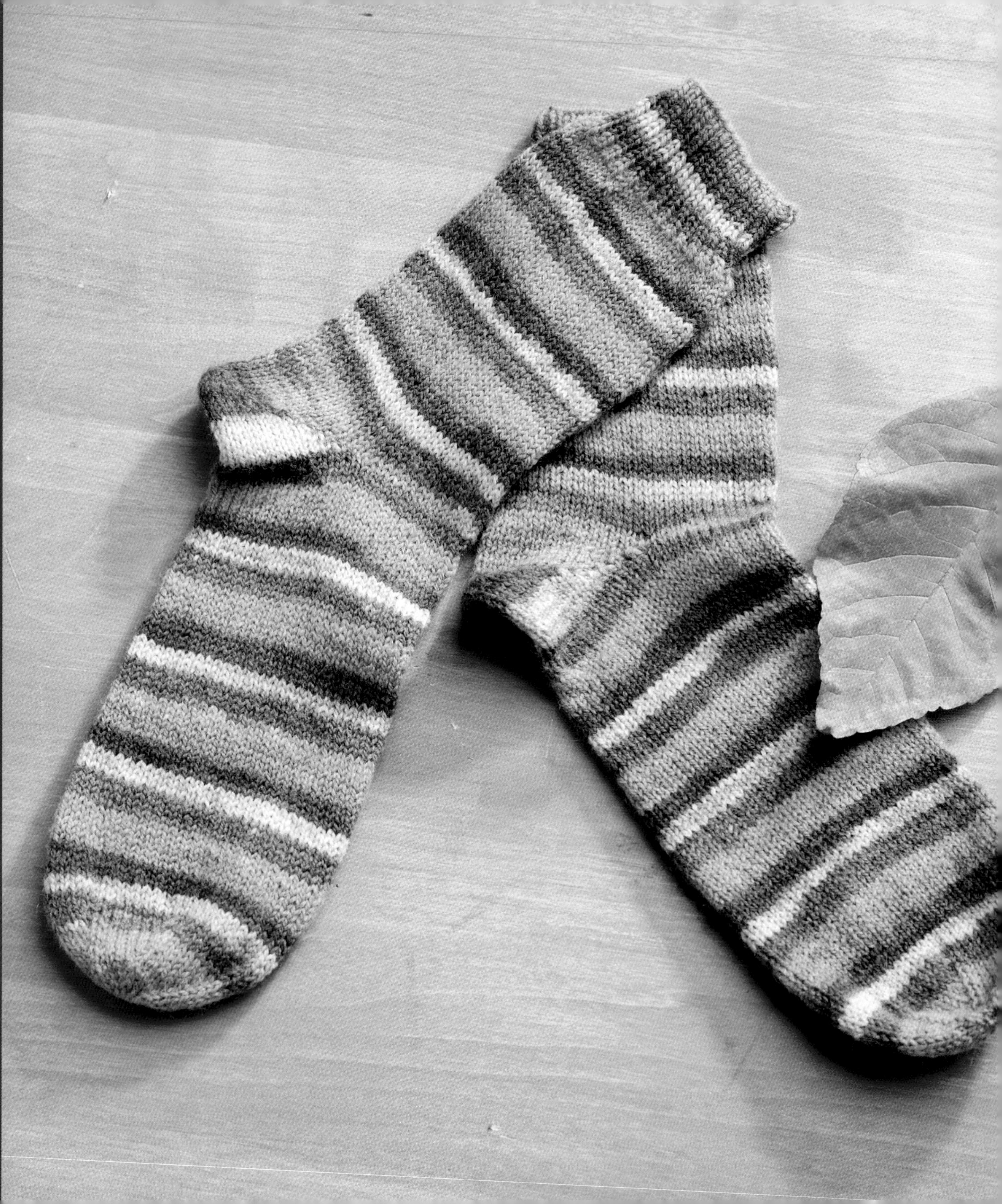

Spring Stripes Socks

By doing your own dyeing, you can knit a pair of striped socks for every season, every mood, and every outfit in your wardrobe.

Finished Size 7½ (7½, 8)" (19 [19, 20.5] cm) foot circumference and 8¾ (9¼, 9¾)" (22 [23.5, 25] cm) long from back of heel to toe. To fit adult women's small (medium, large); about US shoe sizes 6 (7–8, 9–10).

Yarn *Sock- or fingering-weight wool or wool/nylon blend:* about 450 yd (410 m) off-white (all sizes). We used stash yarn.

Needles Size 2 (2.75 mm): set of four double-pointed (dpn). Adjust needle size if necessary to obtain the correct gauge.

Notions Stitch marker (m); tapestry needle.

Gauge 30 sts and 40 rnds = 4" (10 cm) in St st worked in the round.

Socks: Work as for Adult Watermelon Socks on page 64.

Which stitch patterns show off striping yarns?
Garter stitch
Stockinette stitch
Reverse stockinette stitch
All-over ribbing
Ripple stitches (like feather and fan)

Dye-Pattern Palette Stripe #3

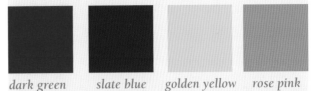

dark green   *slate blue*   *golden yellow*   *rose pink*

Dye Style Stripe.

Dye Rit: dark green, slate blue, golden yellow, and rose pink.

Dye Recipes For each of the slate blue, golden yellow, and rose pink dyes, mix ½ teaspoon (2.5 ml) dye with 2 tablespoons (30 ml) white vinegar and 1 cup (240 ml) hot water. Mix together ¼ teaspoon (1.2 ml) each of dark green dye and slate blue dye with 2 tablespoons (30 ml) white vinegar and 1 cup (240 ml) hot water (to make green/blue). Mix ¼ teaspoon (1.2 ml) of dark green dye with 2 tablespoons (30 ml) white vinegar and 1 cup (240 ml) hot water.

Skein Length 40 feet (12 m).

Dye Pattern Lengths 96" (243 cm) dark green/slate blue; 96" (243 cm) golden yellow; 96" (243 cm) rose; 96" (243 cm) slate blue; remainder very lightly painted with diluted dark green.

Chapter 7

Fair Isle Projects

Self-patterning Fair Isle yarns—what can we say?
Even if you love two-stranded knitting, the magic of
these yarns is sure to entice. And socks, hats, mittens,
and gloves are just more agreeable to knit and wear
without pokey woven-in ends. You get to choose as
many colors as you do for any "real" Fair Isle project.
Painting the yarns is so much fun, and the patterns
that knit up are charming. Enjoy the experience!

Forest Trail Socks

You can never have too many pairs of socks. These, and the Midnight Garden socks, follow the pattern for the Ladies' Watermelon Socks (page 64), just like the socks on pages 66 and 68. Remember that many plain sock patterns are well suited to self-patterning Fair Isle yarns.

Finished Size 7½ (7½, 8)" (19 [19, 20.5] cm) foot circumference and 8¾ (9¼, 9¾)" (22 [23.5, 25] cm) long from back of heel to toe. To fit adult women's small (medium, large); about US shoe sizes 6 (7–8, 9–10).

Yarn *Sock- or fingering-weight wool or wool/nylon blend:* about 450 yd (410 m) off-white (all sizes). We used Brown Sheep Wildfoote Luxury Sock Yarn (75% machine-washable wool, 25% nylon; 215 yd [197 m]/50 g): #SY-10 vanilla, 2 skeins.

Needles Size 2 (2.75 mm): set of four double-pointed (dpn). Adjust needle size if necessary to obtain the correct gauge.

Notions Stitch marker (m); tapestry needle.

Gauge 30 sts and 40 rnds = 4" (10 cm) in St st worked in the round.

Socks: Work as for Adult Watermelon Socks on page 64.

Dye-Pattern Palette Fair Isle # 1

avocado   chestnut   Bermuda sand   raven

Dye Style Fair Isle.

Dyes Country Classics: avocado, chestnut, Bermuda sand, and raven.

Dye Recipes For each of the avocado, Bermuda sand, and chestnut dyes, mix ½ teaspoon (2.5 ml) dye with 2 tablespoons (30 ml) white vinegar and 1 cup (240 ml) hot water. Mix 1 teaspoon (5 ml) raven dye with 2 tablespoons (30 ml) white vinegar and 1 cup (240 ml) hot water.

Skein Length 40 feet (12 m).

First Dye Pattern Lengths 72" (183 cm) avocado; 72" (183 cm) avocado dashes 2" (5 cm) long and with 2" (5-cm) spaces in between; 72" (183 cm) Bermuda sand; 72" (183 cm) undyed; 36" (91.5 cm) chestnut; 72" (183 cm) chestnut dashes 2" (5 cm) long with 2" (5-cm) spaces in between; remainder undyed.

Second Dye Colors Mark the center of the avocado dashes section and paint the second half of those spaces with Bermuda sand. Mark the center of the chestnut dashes section and paint the second half of those spaces with raven.

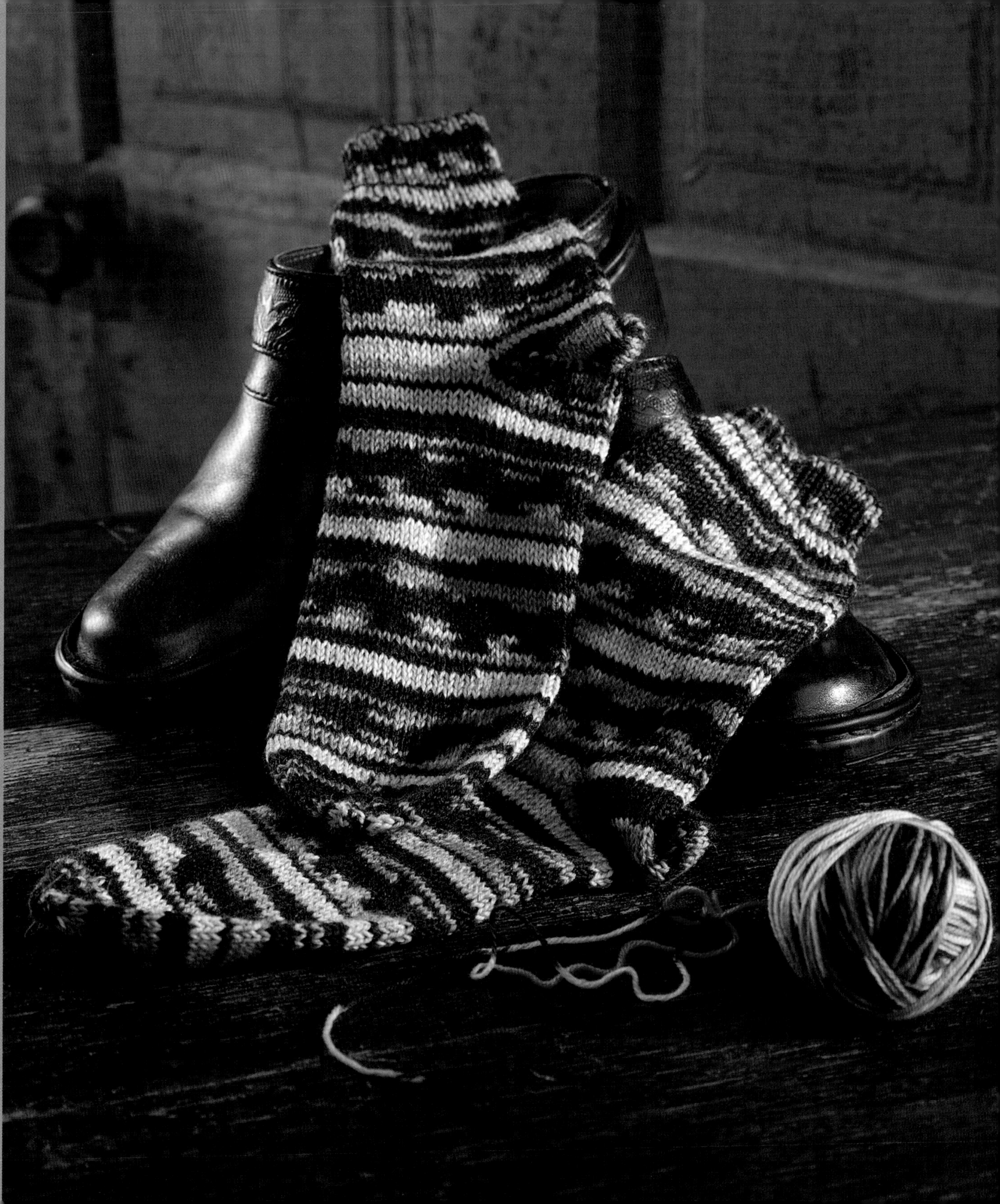

Midnight Garden Socks

Fair Isle tradition meets the colors of modern urban nightlife in these easy-to-knit socks.

Finished Size 7½ (7½, 8)" (19 [19, 20.5] cm) foot circumference and 8¾ (9¼, 9¾)" (22 [23.5, 25] cm) long from back of heel to toe. To fit adult women's small (medium, large); about US shoe sizes 6 (7–8, 9–10).

Yarn *Sock- or fingering-weight wool or wool/nylon blend*: about 450 yd (410 m) off-white (all sizes). We used Brown Sheep Wildfoote Luxury Sock Yarn (75% machine-washable wool, 25% nylon; 215 yd [197 m]/50 g): #SY-10 vanilla, 2 skeins.

Needles Size 2 (2.75 mm): set of four double-pointed (dpn). Adjust needle size if necessary to obtain the correct gauge.

Notions Stitch marker (m); tapestry needle.

Gauge 30 sts and 40 rnds = 4" (10 cm) in St st worked in the round.

Socks: Work as for Adult Watermelon Socks on page 64.

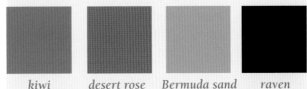

Dye-Pattern Palette Fair Isle #2

kiwi   desert rose   Bermuda sand   raven

Dye Style Fair Isle.

Dyes Country Classics: kiwi, desert rose, Bermuda sand, and raven.

Dye Recipes For each of the kiwi, desert rose, and Bermuda sand dyes, mix ½ teaspoon (2.5 ml) dye with 2 tablespoons (30 ml) white vinegar and 1 cup (240 ml) hot water. Mix 1 teaspoon (5 ml) raven dye with 2 tablespoons (30 ml) white vinegar and 1 cup (240 ml) hot water.

Skein Length 40 feet (12 m).

First Dye Pattern Lengths 72" (183 cm) raven; 36" (91.5 cm) kiwi; 72" (183 cm) raven; 36" (91.5 cm) raven dashes 2" (5 cm) long with 2" (5-cm) spaces in between; 72" (183 cm) raven; 72" (183 cm) raven dashes 2" (5 cm) long with 2" (5-cm) spaces in between; 36" (91.5 cm) desert rose; 36" (91.5cm) raven; remainder Bermuda sand.

Second Dye Colors Paint the undyed portions of the short raven dashes section with desert rose. Mark the center of the long raven dashes section; paint the spaces of the first half with Bermuda sand and the second half with kiwi.

Can I adjust small areas of Fair Isle color in a finished item?

You can color individual stitches with fine-tipped permanent markers or fabric pens, but doing so only works if you are darkening light stitches. Read the manufacturer's instructions to see if the fabric pen ink needs to be heat-set.

No-Slip Slipper Socks

Knit comfy, long-wearing slipper socks for kids and grownups. The classic colors will go with almost any daytime outfit, so kick off your shoes the minute you can! And the nonskid soles are easy to apply.

Finished Size Child: 6½" (16.5 cm) foot circumference (all sizes) and 6½ (7, 7½)" (16.5 [18, 19] cm) long from back of heel to toe; to fit about US children's shoe sizes 10 (11½, 13). **Adult**: 7½ (7½, 8)" (19 [19, 20.5] cm) foot circumference and 8½ (9½, 10)" (21.5 [24, 25.5] cm) long from back of heel to toe; to fit about US women's shoe sizes 5 (7, 9).

Yarn *Worsted-weight wool*: about 210 yd (192 m) off-white for child's sizes; about 300 yd (274 m) off-white for adult's sizes. We used Henry's Attic Montana 4/8 Wool (100% wool; 560 yd [512 m]/8 oz): off-white, about 210 yd (192 m) for child's sizes; 300 yd (274 m) for adult's sizes.

Needles Size 5 (3.75 mm): set of 4 double-pointed (dpn). Adjust needle size if necessary to obtain the correct gauge.

Notions Stitch marker (m); tapestry needle; black Plasti Dip (see www.plastidip.com; available through major hardware retailers) or other non-skid surface material for soles; disposable 1" (2.5 cm) foam paintbrush for applying Plasti Dip; 1½" (3.8-cm) wide masking tape; several plastic shopping bags.

Gauge 22½ sts and 32 rnds = 4" (10 cm) in St st worked in the round.

Note: The slipper socks will have less stretch after the nonskid surface material is applied to the soles. Make sure the slippers are long enough to fit, without stretching, before you paint the soles.

Child's Version

The number of stitches is the same for all three sizes; the larger sizes have longer foot lengths.

Leg: With solid-color scarlet yarn, CO 36 sts. Divide sts evenly on 3 dpn. Join for working in the rnd and place marker to indicate beg of rnd (slip marker every rnd). *Next rnd:* *K1, p1; rep from * around. Rep this rnd 11 more times—12 rnds of ribbing completed; ribbing should measure about 1½" (3.8 cm) from beg. Change to Fair Isle yarn and work even in St st (knit all sts every rnd) until piece measures 5" (12.5 cm) from beg.

Heel: Change to scarlet yarn. Arrange sts so there are 18 sts each on 2 dpn. The needle with the working yarn attached is the heel needle; the other needle holds the sts for the instep (to be worked later). Work the 18 heel sts in short-rows as foll:

Short-row 1: Turn and work across sts on WS as foll: Slip (sl) 1, purl to last st on needle, leave last st unworked, turn.

Short-row 2: (RS) Sl 1, knit to last st, leave last st unworked, turn.

Short-row 3: Sl 1, purl to last 2 sts, leave last 2 sts unworked, turn.

Short-row 4: Sl 1, knit to last 2 sts, leave last 2 sts unworked, turn.

Dye-Pattern Palette Fair Isle #3

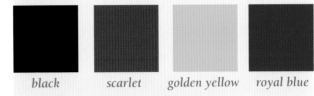

black   scarlet   golden yellow   royal blue

Dye Styles Immersion and Fair Isle.

Dyes Rit: black, scarlet, golden yellow, and royal blue.

Immersion Dye Recipe *Child's version*: Mix 1 teaspoon (5 ml) scarlet dye with ¼ cup (60 ml) white vinegar and 9 cups (2 liters) hot water.

Fair Isle Dye Recipe For each of the scarlet, golden yellow, and royal blue dyes, mix ½ teaspoon (2.5 ml) dye with 2 tablespoons (30 ml) white vinegar and 1 cup (240 ml) hot water. Mix 1 teaspoon (5 ml) black dye with 2 tablespoons (30 ml) white vinegar and 1 cup (240 ml) hot water.

Skein Lengths 40 feet (12 m) for the Fair Isle yarn; 5 feet (1.5 m) for the solid-color yarn.

Special Winding Instructions *Child's version only*: Reserve 80 yd (73 m) of yarn as a 5-foot (1.5-m) skein for immersion dyeing with scarlet.

First Dye Pattern Lengths 36" (91.5 cm) royal blue; 36" (91.5 cm) black; 36" (91.5 cm) black dashes 2" (5 cm) long with 2" (5-cm) spaces in between; 36" (91.5 cm) golden yellow; 36" (91.5 cm) black; 36" (91.5 cm) scarlet; 72" (183 cm) black dashes 2" (5 cm) long with 2" (5-cm) spaces in between; 36" (91.5 cm) scarlet; 36" (91.5 cm) black; 36" (91.5 cm) royal blue; remainder black.

Second Dye Colors Paint the spaces between the black dashes on the short section with royal blue; paint the spaces between the black dashes on the long section with alternating golden yellow and scarlet.

Solid Color Dyes Immersion-dye the reserved yarn with scarlet for child's version.

Cont in this manner, leaving 1 more st unworked at the end of the needle every row before turning, until there are 5 unworked at each end of needle (there will be 8 sts in the center), ending with a RS (knit) row.

Turning-row 1: (WS) Sl 1, p7, sl next st, lift strand between the needles onto left needle by inserting left needle tip under the strand from back to front, return slipped st to left needle, p2tog (slipped st and lifted strand), turn.

Turning-row 2: Sl 1, k8, sl next st, M1 (see Glossary, page 100), pass slipped st over (psso), turn.

Turning-row 3: Sl 1, p9, sl next st, lift strand between needles onto left needle as in Turning-row 1, return slipped st to left needle, p2tog (slipped st and lifted strand), turn.

Turning-row 4: Sl 1, k10, sl next st, M1, psso, turn.

Cont in this manner, working 1 more st every row before slipping next st, until all of the sts have been worked—18 sts on heel needle.

Cont in this manner, working 1 more st every row before slipping the next st, until all of the sts have been worked—18 sts on heel needle.

Foot: Change to Fair Isle yarn. Divide sts evenly on 3 dpn. Work even in St st on all sts until foot measures 5 (5½, 6)" (12.5 [14, 15] cm) from center back heel, or about 1½" (3.8 cm) less than desired total length.

Toe: Change to scarlet yarn. Arrange sts so that there are 9 sts on the first dpn, 18 sts on the second dpn, and 9 sts on the third dpn. Knit 1 rnd. Cont as foll:

Rnd 1: On first needle, knit to last 2 sts, k2tog; on second needle, k2tog, knit to last 2 sts, k2tog; on third needle, k2tog, knit to end—4 sts dec'd; 1 st dec'd each on first and third needles, 2 sts dec'd on second needle.

Rnd 2: Knit.

Rep the last 2 rnds 5 more times—12 sts rem. Cut yarn, leaving a 12" (30.5-cm) tail. Arrange sts evenly on 2 dpn with the 6 top-of-foot sts on 1 needle and the 6 sole sts on the other dpn. Thread tail on tapestry needle and use the Kitchener stitch (see Glossary, page 98)

to graft sts tog. Weave in ends. See directions on page 79 for applying the non-stick sole material.

Adult's Version

Leg: With Fair Isle yarn, CO 42 (42, 46) sts. Divide sts as evenly as possible on 3 dpn. Join for working in the rnd and place marker to indicate beg of rnd (slip marker every rnd). *Next rnd:* *K1, p1; rep from * around. Rep this rnd 14 more times—15 rnds of ribbing completed; ribbing should measure about 2" (5 cm) from beg. Work even in St st (knit all sts every rnd) until piece measures 8" (20.5 cm) from beg.

Heel: Divide sts on 2 dpn with 20 (20, 22) sts on one needle and 22 (22, 24) sts on the other. The needle with 22 (22, 24) sts is the heel needle; the other needle holds the sts for the instep (to be worked later). Work the 22 (22, 24) heel sts in short-rows as foll:

Short-row 1: Turn and work across sts on WS as foll: Slip (sl) 1, purl to last st on heel needle, leave last st unworked, turn.

Short-row 2: (RS) Sl 1, knit to last st, leave last st unworked, turn.

Short-row 3: Sl 1, purl to last 2 sts, leave last 2 sts unworked, turn.

Short-row 4: Sl 1, knit to last 2 sts, leave last 2 sts unworked, turn.

Cont in this manner, leaving 1 more st unworked at the end of the needle every row before turning, until there are 7 (7, 8) sts unworked at each end of needle (there will be 8 sts in the center), ending with a RS (knit) row.

Turning-row 1: (WS) Sl 1, p7, sl next st, lift strand between the needles onto left needle by inserting left needle tip under the strand from back to front, return slipped st to left needle, p2tog (slipped st and lifted strand), turn.

Turning-row 2: Sl 1, k8, sl next st, M1 (see Glossary, page 100), pass slipped st over (psso), turn.

Turning-row 3: Sl 1, p9, sl next st, lift strand between needles onto left needle as in Turning-row 1, return slipped st to left needle, p2tog (slipped st and lifted strand), turn.

Turning-row 4: Sl 1, k10, sl next st, M1, psso, turn.

Cont in this manner, working 1 more st every row before slipping next st, until all of the sts have been worked—18 sts on heel needle.

Cont in this manner, working 1 more st every row before slipping next st, until all of the sts have been worked—22 (22, 24) sts on heel needle.

Foot: Divide sts as evenly as possible on 3 dpn. Work even in St st on all sts until piece measures 6¾ (7½, 8)" (17 [19, 20.5] cm) from center back heel, or about 1¾ (1¾, 2)" (4.5 [4.5, 5] cm) less than desired total length.

Toe: Arrange sts on 3 dpn so that there are 10 (10, 12) sts on the first needle, 21 (21, 23) sts on the second needle, and 11 (11, 11) sts on the third needle. Knit 1 rnd. Dec for toe as foll:

Rnd 1: On first needle, knit to last 2 sts, k2tog; on second needle, k2tog, knit to last 2 sts, k2tog; on third needle, k2tog, knit to end—4 sts dec'd; 1 st dec'd each on first and third needles, 2 sts dec'd on second needle.

Rnd 2: Knit.

Rep the last 2 rnds 6 (6, 7) more times—14 sts rem for all sizes. Cut yarn, leaving a 12" (30.5-cm) tail. Arrange sts evenly on 2 dpn with 6 (6, 7) top-of-foot sts on one needle and 6 (6, 7) sole sts on the other. Thread tail on tapestry needle and use the Kitchener stitch (see Glossary, page 99) to graft sts tog. Weave in ends. See directions at right for applying the non-stick sole material.

Applying the Non-Stick Sole

Stuff the slipper foot firmly and smoothly with wadded-up plastic bags. Mark off the sole area with masking tape. Work in a well-ventilated area following the Plasti Dip instructions (or manufacturer's directions if you're using another product). Use a disposable foam paintbrush to apply the coating to the sole of the stuffed slipper sock with a pouncing motion (dabbing briskly up and down, not painting in strokes). Pounce over the edge of the masking tape to achieve a clean outline, and apply the coating evenly but not too heavily. Allow the first coat to dry for 30 minutes, storing the paintbrush in a zippered plastic bag between coats so it doesn't dry out. Apply a second coat and allow to dry for 4 hours. Carefully remove the plastic-bag stuffing and masking tape. Allow the sole to dry another 24 hours before wearing. Dispose of the foam paintbrush.

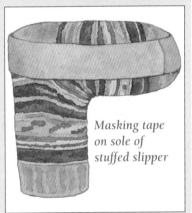

Masking tape on sole of stuffed slipper

no-slip slipper socks

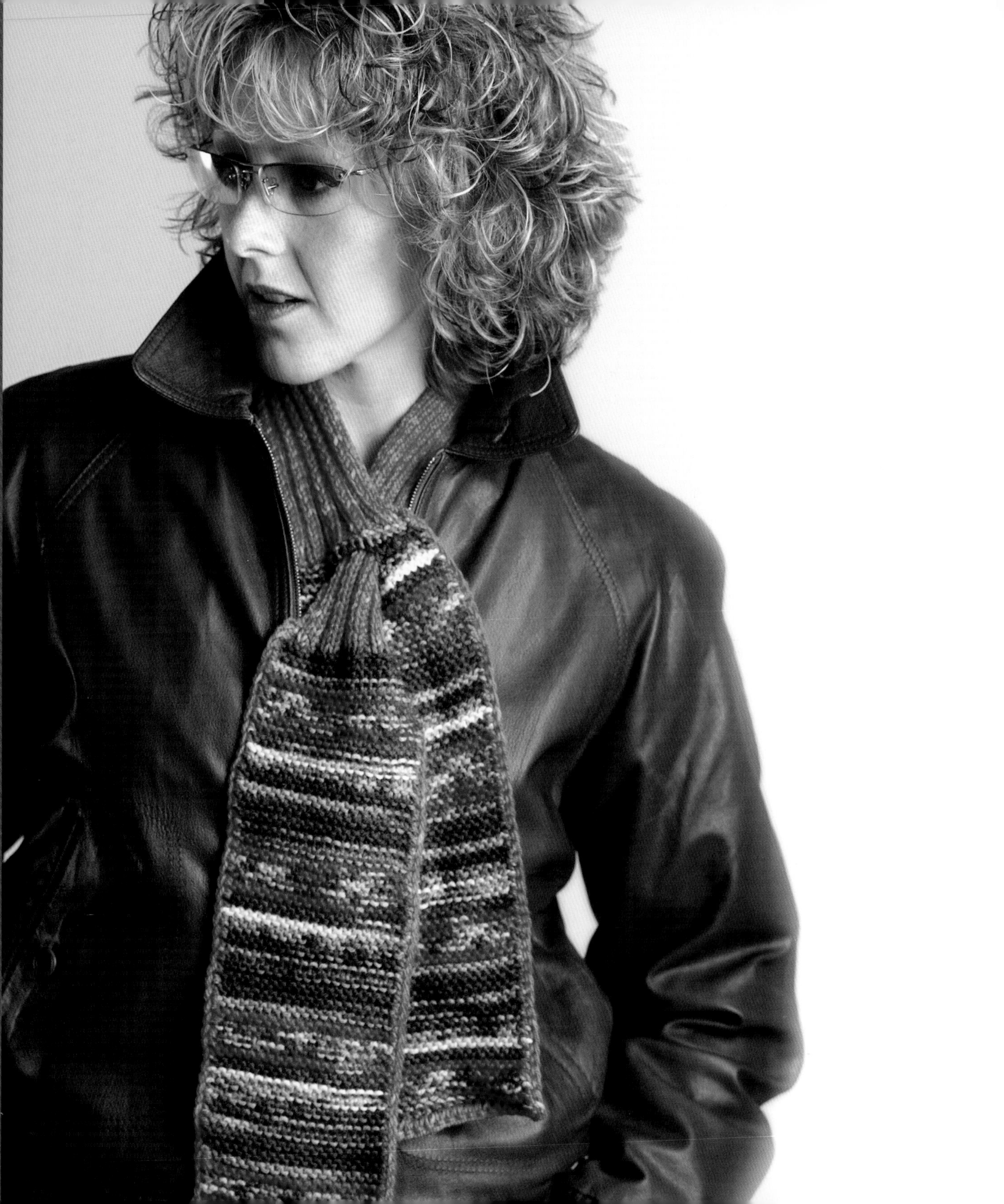

Keyhole Scarf

This versatile little scarf knits up quickly. We used yarn left over from the child's slipper socks (page 77), but you can dye the scarf yarn separately—or use yarn left over from other projects.

Finished Size About 46" (117 cm) long and 4¾" (12 cm) wide at the ends, including crocheted border.

Yarn *Worsted-weight wool*: about 170 yd (155 m) off-white. We used Henry's Attic Montana 4/8 Wool (100% wool; 560 yd [512 m]/8 oz): off-white, about 170 yd (155 m). The sample shown uses about 110 yd (100 m) Fair Isle yarn, and 60 yd (55 m) of solid-color yarn left-over from the No-Slip Slipper Socks project on page 77.

Needles Size 8 (5 mm): straight. Adjust needle size if necessary to obtain the correct gauge.

Notions Tapestry needle; size G (4.5 mm) crochet hook.

Gauge 18½ sts and 32 rows = 4" (10 cm) in garter st.

Scarf

With Fair Isle yarn, CO 20 sts. Work in garter st (knit all sts every row) until piece measures 12½" (31.5 cm) from beg.

Keyhole: On the next row, k7, BO center 6 sts, k7. Knit across the foll row, using the backward loop method (see Glossary, page 99) to CO 6 sts over gap in the previous row to complete keyhole—20 sts.

Neck ribbing: Change to Scarlet yarn. *Next row:* *K2,

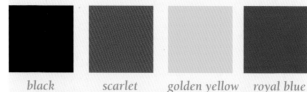

| black | scarlet | golden yellow | royal blue |

If you're using new yarn, dye 110 yd (100 m) Fair Isle yarn, and 60 yd (55 m) of solid color yarn as for Slipper Socks on page 77.

p2; rep from * to end. Rep this row until ribbing section measures about 20" (51 cm), or scarf measures about 32½" (82.5 cm) from beg. Change to Fair Isle yarn. Work in garter st until second garter st section measures 12½" (31.5 cm), or piece measures about 45" (114.5 cm) from beg. BO all sts.

Crochet border: With scarlet yarn and crochet hook, beg at one edge where garter st meets ribbing, work 1 row of single crochet (sc; see Glossary, page 100, for crochet instructions) all around the scarf, working 3 sc into each corner. Join to beg with a slip st.

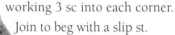

Cut yarn and fasten off. Weave in ends. To wear, place scarf around neck and thread one end through the keyhole.

keyhole scarf

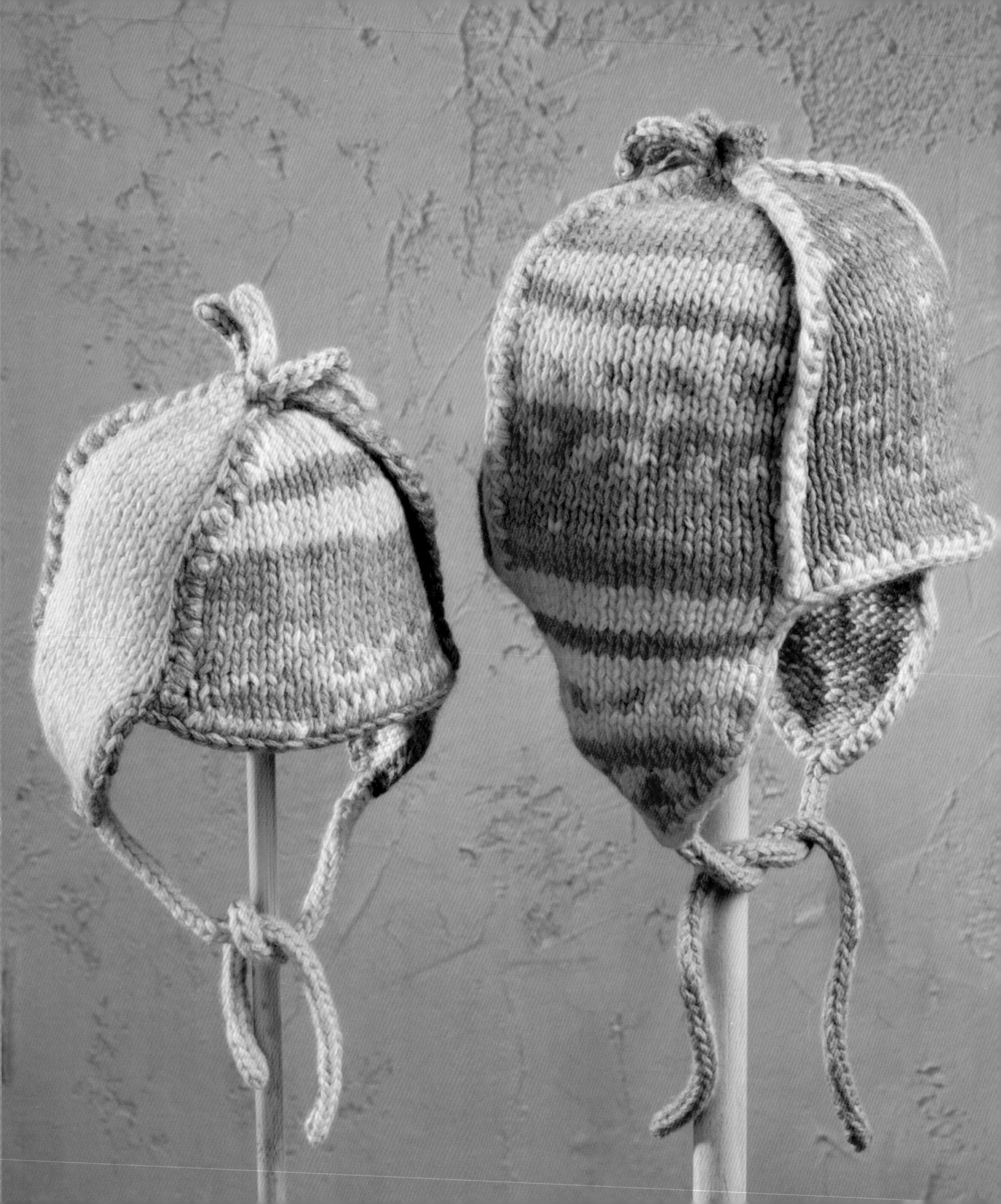

Tassel-Top Earflap Hats

Soft yarn and muted colors make for a beautiful pair of children's hats. The angora blend yarn and earflaps will protect tykes against the bitterest winter weather.

Finished Size 16 (19½)" (40.5 [49.5] cm) head circumference and 5 (6¾)" (12.5 [17] cm) tall, not including ties and earflaps. To fit infant (child).

Yarn Worsted-weight angora/wool or angora/wool/nylon blend: about 390 yd (357 m) off-white. We used Berroco Pleasure (66% angora, 29% merino wool, 5% nylon; 130 yd [119 m]/50 g): #8602 blizzard (off-white), 3 skeins for both hats.

Needles Size 9 (5.5 mm): set of 4 double-pointed (dpn). Adjust needle size if necessary to obtain the correct gauge.

Notions Tapestry needle; size G (4.5 mm) crochet hook.

Gauge 18 sts and 27 rows = 4" (10 cm) in St st.

Earflap Panels (**make 2**)

With maize yarn for infant's hat or Fair Isle yarn for child's hat, CO 3 sts for both sizes. Work I-cord (see Glossary, page 99) until piece measures 7 (8)" (18 [20.5] cm) from beg. Cont as foll:

Row 1: (RS) Using the backward loop method (see Glossary, page 98), CO 1 st, knit to end, pick up and knit 1 st from base of last st—2 sts inc'd.

Row 2: Purl.

Rep the last 2 rows 5 (7) more times—15 (19) sts. Work St st back and forth in rows (knit all sts on RS rows,

Dye-Pattern Palette Fair Isle #4

blueberry   desert rose   maize

Dye Styles Immersion and Fair Isle.

Dyes Country Classics: blueberry, desert rose, and maize.

Immersion Dye Recipe Mix 1 teaspoon (5 ml) blueberry dye with ¾ cup (180 ml) white vinegar and 9 cups (2 liters) hot water. Mix ½ teaspoon (2.5 ml) maize dye with ¾ cup (180 ml) white vinegar and 9 cups (2 liters) hot water.

Fair Isle Dye Recipe For each of the blueberry and desert rose dyes, mix ½ teaspoon (2.5 ml) dye with 2 tablespoons (30 ml) white vinegar and 1 cup (240 ml) hot water. Mix ¼ teaspoon (1.2 ml) maize dye with 2 tablespoons (30 ml) white vinegar and 1 cup (240 ml) hot water.

Skein Lengths 40 feet (12 m) for the Fair Isle yarn; 5 feet (1.5 m) for the solid-color yarn.

Special Dyeing Instructions Wind two 130-yd (119-m) 5-foot (1.5-m) skeins, wet the skeins, then immersion-dye one skein each of maize and blueberry; wind remaining yarn into a 40-foot (12-m) skein and dye as per the Fair Isle directions. *Note:* If you want to knit only one hat, dye one 130-yd (119-m) skein in the solid color and one 130-yd (119-m) skein in the Fair Isle pattern.

Dye Pattern Lengths: 72" (183 cm) desert rose; 36" (91.5 cm) blueberry; 36" (91.5 cm) desert rose; 36" (91.5 cm) desert rose dashes 2" (5 cm) long with 2" (5-cm) spaces in between; 36" (91.5 cm) desert rose; 36" (91.5 cm) maize; 36" (91.5 cm) blueberry dashes 2" (5 cm) long with 2" (5-cm) spaces in between; 36" (91.5 cm) undyed; 36" (91.5 cm) desert rose; remainder maize.

Finishing

Hold one earflap panel and front panel tog with WS of each piece touching. With blueberry yarn for infant's hat or maize yarn for child's hat, use crochet hook to join pieces together with single crochet (sc; see Glossary, page 100, for crochet instructions), working down from the I-cord topknots to the CO edge of front panel. Join back panel in the same way to other side of the same earflap panel. Join the rem earflap panel in the same way between front and back panels. With blueberry yarn for infant's hat or maize yarn for child's hat, work 1 row of sc all around the lower edge of the hat, including ear flaps, working 2 sc in same st at lower point of each ear flap. Join to beg with a slip st. Cut yarn and fasten off last st. With yarn threaded on a tapestry needle, sew base of topknot I-cords tog to close top of hat. Weave in ends.

Wee Winter Mittens

With yarn left over from the Earflap Hats, you can knit soft, matching mittens for little hands. You can also dye the yarn for this project independently—and, if an angora blend is too warm for your climate, you might experiment with merino wool.

Finished Size 6" (15 cm) hand circumference and 6½" (16.5 cm) long from base of cuff to tip. To fit a small child.

Yarn *Worsted-weight angora/wool or angora/wool/nylon blend:* about 111 yd (102 m) off-white. We used Berroco Pleasure (66% angora, 29% merino wool, 5% nylon; 130 yd [119 m]/50 g): #8602 blizzard (off-white), 1 skein (both sizes). The sample shown uses about 75 yd (69 m) Fair Isle yarn and 36 yd (33 m) of solid-color yarn leftover from the Earflap Hats project.

purl all sts on WS rows) until piece measures 4 (6)" (10 [15] cm) from last inc row—piece should measure about 5¾ (8¼)" (14.5 [21] cm) from top of I-cord tie. Cont as foll:

Row 1: K2tog, knit to last 2 sts, k2tog—2 sts dec'd.
Row 2: Purl.

Rep the last 2 rows 5 (7) more times—3 sts rem (both sizes). Work rem sts in I-cord 1½ (2)" (3.8 [5] cm) from last dec row for topknot. K3tog—1 st rem. Cut yarn, leaving a 12" (30.5-cm) tail. Thread tail on tapestry needle and draw through rem st to fasten off. Weave ends into the center of each I-cord tube.

Front and Back Panels (make 2)

With Fair Isle yarn for infant's hat or blueberry yarn for child's hat, CO 21 (25) sts. Work in St st back and forth in rows until piece measures 2½ (3¼)" (6.5 [8.5] cm) from beg, ending with a WS row.

Row 1: K2tog, knit to last 2 sts, k2tog—2 sts dec'd.
Row 2: Purl.

Rep the last 2 rows 8 (10) more times—3 sts rem. Work rem sts in I-cord for 1½" (3.8 cm) from last dec row for topknot. K3tog—1 st rem. Cut yarn, leaving a 12" (30.5-cm) tail. Thread tail on tapestry needle and draw through rem st to fasten off. Weave ends into the center of the I-cord tubes.

Needles Size 8 (5 mm): set of 4 double-pointed (dpn). Adjust needle size if necessary to obtain the correct gauge.

Notion Stitch marker (m); 2 safety pins or 1 stitch holder; tapestry needle.

Gauge 20 sts and 30½ rnds = 4" (10 cm) in St st worked in the round.

Mittens (make 2)

Cuff: With solid-color yarn, CO 30 sts. Divide sts evenly on 3 dpn. Join for working in the rnd and place marker (pm) to indicate beg of rnd (slip marker every rnd). *Next rnd:* *K1, p1; rep from * around. Rep this rnd 11 more times—12 rnds of ribbing completed; cuff should measure about 2¼" (5.5 cm) from beg. Change to Fair Isle yarn.

Thumb gusset: Knit 4 rnds. Cont as foll:

Rnd 1: (Inc rnd) M1 (see Glossary, page 100), k1, M1, pm, knit to end—32 sts; 3 gusset sts between markers.

Rnd 2: Knit.

Rnd 3: (Inc rnd) M1, knit to next m, M1, slip marker, knit to end—2 sts inc'd between the markers.

Rnd 4: Knit.

Rep the last 2 rnds 3 more times—40 sts; 11 gusset sts between markers.

Hand: Place the 11 gusset sts on a stitch holder (or divide sts on 2 safety pins to make it easier to try on the mitten) to work later for thumb, use the backward loop method (see Glossary, page 99) to CO 1 st over the gap, knit to end—30 sts. Knit 11 rnds even—piece should measure about 5½" (14 cm) from beg, or to tip of little finger.

Shape top: Cont as foll:

Rnd 1: *K3, k2tog; rep from * around—24 sts rem.

Rnds 2, 4, and 6: Knit.

Rnd 3: *K2, k2tog; rep from * around—18 sts rem.

blueberry	*desert rose*	*maize*

If you're using new yarn, dye 75 yd (69 m) Fair Isle yarn and 36 yd (33 m) of solid-color yarn as for Ear Flap Hats on page 83.

Rnd 5: *K1, k2tog; rep from * around—12 sts rem.

Rnd 7: *K2 tog; rep from * around—6 sts rem.

Cut yarn, leaving a 12" (30.5-cm) tail. Thread tail on tapestry needle and draw through rem sts. Pull snugly to close mitten tip, and fasten off on inside.

Thumb: Place 11 held gusset sts as evenly as possible on 3 dpn. Join yarn to end of sts with RS facing. Pick up and knit 1 st from the base of the st CO over the gap in the hand, knit to end—12 sts. Knit 5 rnds even. *Next rnd:* *K2tog; rep from * around—6 sts rem. Cut yarn, leaving a 12" (30.5-cm) tail. Thread tail on tapestry needle and draw through rem sts. Pull snugly to close thumb tip, and fasten off on inside. Weave in ends.

wee winter mittens

Asymmetrical Vest

Self-patterning yarn isn't just for small projects! Considering how much fun you can have dyeing these yarns and knitting this vest, the finished product is marvelously sophisticated.

Finished Size 38 (42, 47)" (96.5 [106.5, 119.5] cm) chest/bust circumference. To fit adult women's small (medium, large).

Yarn *Worsted-weight wool*: about 1115 (1115, 1338) yd [1020 (1020, 1224) m] white. We used Patons Classic Merino Wool (100% wool; 223 yd [204 m]/100 g): #201 winter white, 5 (5, 6) balls.

Needles Size 7 (4.5 mm): straight. Adjust needle size if necessary to obtain the correct gauge.

Notions Tapestry needle; size G (4.5 mm) crochet hook; three 1¼" (3.2-cm) wooden toggle-style buttons; sewing needle and matching thread for attaching buttons.

Gauge 19½ sts and 27 rows = 4" (10 cm) in St st.

Note: The vest is worked in stockinette stitch from side-to-side in one piece, beginning at the right front opening, working around the back, and ending at the left front opening. The sample shown is the smallest size; the Fair Isle patterning will appear differently on the other two sizes because they are worked over a larger number of stitches.

Dye-Pattern Palette Fair Isle #5

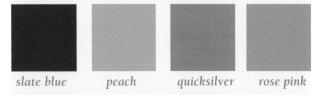

slate blue   peach   quicksilver   rose pink

Dye Styles Immersion and Fair Isle.

Dyes Rit: slate blue, peach, and rose pink; Country Classics: quicksilver.

Immersion Dye Recipe For each of the slate blue and quicksilver dyes, mix 1 teaspoon (5 ml) dye with ¾ cup (180 ml) white vinegar and 12 cups (3 liters) hot water. For each of the peach and rose pink dyes, mix ½ teaspoon (2.5 ml) dye with ½ cup (120 ml) white vinegar and 6 cups (1.5 liters) hot water.

Fair Isle Dye Recipes For each of the rose pink and peach dyes, mix ½ teaspoon (2.5 ml) dye with 2 tablespoons (30 ml) white vinegar and 1 cup (240 ml) hot water. For each of the slate blue and quicksilver dyes, mix 1 teaspoon (5 ml) dye with 2 tablespoons (30 ml) white vinegar and 1 cup (240 ml) hot water.

Skein Lengths 5 feet (1.5 m) for immersion skeins; 40 feet (12 m) for Fair Isle skeins.

continued on page 88

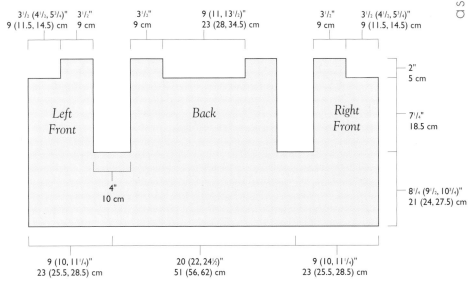

3½ (4½, 5¾)" 9 (11.5, 14.5) cm   3½" 9 cm   3½" 9 cm   9 (11, 13½)" 23 (28, 34.5) cm   3½" 9 cm   3½ (4½, 5¾)" 9 (11.5, 14.5) cm

2" 5 cm

7¼" 18.5 cm

8¼ (9½, 10¾)" 21 (24, 27.5) cm

Left Front   Back   Right Front

4" 10 cm

9 (10, 11¼)" 23 (25.5, 28.5) cm   20 (22, 24½)" 51 (56, 62) cm   9 (10, 11¼)" 23 (25.5, 28.5) cm

Special Dyeing Instructions Wind two 110-yd (100-m) 40-foot (12-m) skeins for Fair Isle dyeing (all sizes). Wind 223 yd (204 m) of yarn into a 5-foot (1.5 m) skein for immersion dyeing with quicksilver (all sizes). Wind 110-yd (100-m) of yarn into two 5-foot (1.5-m) skeins for immersion dyeing—one each of peach and rose pink (all sizes). For small and medium sizes, wind 333 yd (304 m) of yarn into a 5-foot (1.5-m) skein for immersion dyeing with slate blue. For large size, wind two 223-yd (204-m) of yarn into 5-foot (1.5-m) skeins for immersion dyeing with slate blue.

Dye Pattern Lengths Divide each 40-foot (12-m) skein into two 20-foot (6-m) sections; mark the divisions by tying on contrasting yarn. **Quicksilver/Peach Fair Isle Skein:** Paint half of the skein with quicksilver dye. Paint the other half with quicksilver dashes 1" (2.5 cm) long with 3" (7.5-cm) spaces in between. Heat-set the skein. In the second-stage dyeing, paint the remaining spaces with peach. **Slate Blue/Rose Pink Fair Isle Skein:** Paint as above but use slate blue as the main color and rose pink for the spaces.

Right Front

With immersion-dyed peach, CO 76 (82, 88) sts. Work even in St st (knit all sts on RS, purl all sts on WS) for 4 rows, ending with a WS row. Cut peach and join quicksilver/peach Fair Isle, beg at a quicksilver section. Work even for 8 (12, 16) rows. Cut Fair Isle and join immersion-dyed quicksilver. Work even for 1 row. Cut quicksilver and join quicksilver/peach Fair Isle, beg at a Fair Isle section. Work even for 8 (12, 16) rows. Cut Fair Isle and join immersion-dyed peach. Work even for 2 rows, ending with a RS row—23 (31, 39) rows completed; piece should measure about 3½ (4½, 5¾)" (9 [11.5, 14.5] cm) from beg.

Right front neck: (WS) Cut peach yarn and join immersion-dyed quicksilver. Purl next row, then use the backward loop method (see Glossary, page 99) to CO 10 sts at the end of the row (neck edge)—86 (92, 98) sts. Work even for 6 more rows. Cut quicksilver and join immersion-dyed peach. Work 2 rows peach, 2 rows slate blue, then 2 rows peach. Cut peach and join immersion-dyed quicksilver. Work even for 10 rows, ending with a WS row—piece should measure about 7 (8, 9¼)" (18 [20.5, 23.5] cm) from beg; shoulder should measure 3½" (9 cm) from neck CO.

Right front armhole: At beg of next row (RS), BO 46 sts, work to end—40 (46, 52) sts rem. Work even for 2" (5 cm). Mark last row worked with a piece of scrap yarn to indicate position of side.

Back

Work even for 2" (5 cm) beyond marker, ending with a RS row—piece should measure about 11 (12, 13¼)" (28 [30.5, 33.5] cm) from beg.

Right back armhole: (WS) Purl next row, then use the backward loop method to CO 46 sts at the end of the row—86 (92, 98) sts. Work even for 10 more rows. Cut quicksilver and join immersion-dyed peach. Work 2 rows peach, 2 rows slate blue, then 2 rows peach. Cut peach and join immersion-dyed quicksilver. Work 6 rows even, ending with a WS row—piece should measure about 14½ (15½, 16¾)" (37 [39.5, 42.5] cm) from beg; right back shoulder should measure 3½" (9 cm) from sts CO for armhole.

Right back neck: At beg of next row (RS), BO 10 sts, work to end—76 (82, 88) sts rem. Cut quicksilver and join immersion-dyed peach. Work even for 2 rows. Cut peach and join quicksilver/peach Fair Isle, beg at a quicksilver section. Work even for 8 (12, 16) rows. Cut Fair Isle and join immersion-dyed quicksilver. Work 1 row. Cut quicksilver and join quicksilver/peach Fair Isle, beg at a Fair Isle section. Work even for 8 (12, 16) rows. Cut Fair Isle and join immersion-dyed peach. Work even for 2 rows, ending with a WS row—piece should measure about 17¾ (20, 22½)" (45 [51, 57] cm) from beg. Cut peach and join immersion-dyed slate blue. Work even until piece measures 20½ (22¼, 24¾)" (52 [56.5, 63] cm) from beg, or about 6 (6¾, 8) (15 [17, 20.5] cm) from sts BO for right back neck, ending with a WS row. Cut slate blue and join immersion-dyed rose pink. Work even for 2 rows. Cut rose pink and join slate blue/rose pink Fair Isle, beg at a slate blue section. Work even for 8 (12, 16) rows. Cut Fair Isle and join immersion-dyed slate blue. Work even for 1 row. Cut slate blue and join slate blue/rose pink Fair Isle, beg with a Fair Isle section. Work even for 8 (12, 16) rows. Cut Fair Isle and join immersion-dyed rose pink. Work even for 2 rows, ending with a RS row—piece should measure about 23½ (26½, 30¼)" (59.5 [67.5, 77] cm) from beg; neck opening should measure about 9 (11, 13½)" (23 [28, 34.5] cm) from sts BO for right back neck. Cut rose pink and join immersion-dyed slate blue.

Left back neck: (WS) Purl next row then use backward loop method to CO 10 sts at end of row (neck edge)—86 (92, 98) sts. Work even for 23 more rows, ending with a WS row—left back shoulder should measure about 3½" (9 cm) from sts CO for neck.

Left back armhole: On next row (RS), BO 46 sts, work to end—40 (46, 52) sts rem. Cut slate blue and join immersion-dyed quicksilver. Work even for 2" (5 cm). Mark last row worked with a piece of scrap yarn to indicate position of side.

Left Front

Work even for another 2" (5 cm) beyond marker, ending with a RS row—piece should measure about 31 (34, 37¾)" (78.5 [86.5, 96] cm) from beg. Cut quicksilver and join immersion-dyed slate blue.

Left front armhole: (WS) Purl next row, then use backward loop method to CO 46 sts at end of row—86 (92, 98) sts. Work even for 23 more rows, ending with a WS row—shoulder should measure about 3½" (9 cm) from sts CO for armhole.

Left front neck: On next row (RS), BO 10 sts, work to end—76 (82, 88) sts rem. Work 1 row even. Cut slate blue and join immersion-dyed rose pink. Work even for 2 rows. Cut rose pink and join slate blue/rose pink Fair Isle, beg at a slate blue section. Work even for 8 (12, 16) rows. Cut Fair Isle and join immersion-dyed slate blue. Work even for 1 row. Cut slate blue and join slate blue/rose pink Fair Isle, beg with a Fair Isle section. Work even for 8 (12, 16) rows. Cut Fair Isle and join immersion-dyed rose pink. Work even for 2 rows, ending with a RS row—piece should measure about 38 (42, 47)" (96.5 [106.5, 119.5] cm) from beg; neck opening should measure about 3½ (4½, 5¾)" (9 [11.5, 14.5] cm) from sts BO for left front neck. BO all sts.

Finishing

With yarn threaded on a tapestry needle, sew front and back tog at shoulders, matching stripe patt on right shoulder.

Lower border: With immersion-dyed slate blue and crochet hook, RS facing, beg at lower edge of left front, work 1 row single crochet (sc; see Glossary, page 100, for crochet instructions) around lower edge of vest. Turn. *Next row:* Chain (ch) 1, work 1 sc in each sc across, turn. Rep the last row 4 more times—6 sc rows completed. Cut yarn and fasten off last st.

Left front border: With immersion-dyed slate blue and crochet hook, RS facing, beg at neck edge of left front, work 1 row of sc along left front opening. Turn. *Next row:* Ch 1, work 1 sc in each sc across, turn. Rep the last row 2 more times—4 sc rows completed. Cut yarn and fasten off last st.

Right front border: Beg at lower edge of right front with RS facing, work as for left front border.

Neck edging and button loops: On right front, mark position of 3 evenly spaced button loops, the highest about 2½" (6.5 cm) down from neck edge, the lowest about 1" (2.5 cm) below beg of armhole shaping, and the third halfway between. With immersion-dyed slate blue, crochet hook, RS facing, and beg at lower left front corner, work 1 sc in each sc around lower edge of vest, work 3 sc in lower right front corner, work 1 sc in each sc up right front, making button loops opposite markers as foll: *Work to marked position, ch 8, sc in next sc of border to close loop; rep from * 2 more times—3 button loops completed. Work sc to top of right front, work 3 sc in corner, work sc around neck opening to top of left front, work 3 sc in corner, work 1 sc in each sc of left front to end. Join with a slip st in first sc. Cut yarn and fasten off.

Armhole edging: With immersion-dyed slate blue, work 1 row sc evenly around armhole openings, join with a slip st in first sc. Cut yarn and fasten off.

Weave in ends. Sew toggle buttons to left front opposite button loops.

Can I adjust the pattern that develops from a Fair Isle self-patterning yarn as I'm knitting? If you really must make certain pattern elements line up perfectly, you can cut out a section of the yarn and rejoin the yarn at a new place in the pattern repeat.

Carnival Colors Fingerless Gloves

Use fingering-weight yarn for socks—and gloves! These festive mitts leave fingers free for eating funnel cakes or gripping the bars on rides.

Finished Size 5 (5½, 6, 6½)" (12.5 [14, 15, 16.5] cm) hand circumference, unstretched, and 6 (6½, 6¾, 7)" (15 [16.5, 17, 18] cm) long with top edge rolled. To fit a child (women's small, women's medium, women's large). *Note:* These gloves are sized for a very snug fit.

Yarn *Sock- or fingering-weight wool or wool/nylon blend:* about 113 yd (103 m) off-white (all sizes). We used stash yarn.

Needles Size 2 (2.75 mm): set of 4 double-pointed (dpn). Adjust needle size if necessary to obtain the correct gauge.

Notions Stitch markers (m); 2 safety pins or 1 stitch holder; tapestry needle.

Gauge 35 sts and 46 rnds = 4" (10 cm) in St st worked in the round.

Fingerless Gloves (make 2)
Cuff: CO 44 (48, 52, 56) sts. Divide as evenly as possible on 3 dpn. Join for working in the rnd and place marker (pm) to indicate beg of rnd (slip marker every rnd). *Next rnd:* *K2, p2; rep from * around. Rep this rnd 29 more times—30 rnds of ribbing completed; cuff should measure about 2½" (6.5 cm) from beg.

Dye-Pattern Palette Fair Isle #5

very hot pink	blueberry	maize	raven

Dye Style Fair Isle.

Dyes Country Classics: very hot pink, blueberry, maize, and raven.

Dye Recipes For each of the hot pink, blueberry, and maize dyes, mix ½ teaspoon (2.5 ml) dye with 2 tablespoons (30 ml) white vinegar and 1 cup (240 ml) hot water. Mix 1 teaspoon (5 ml) raven dye with 2 tablespoons (30 ml) white vinegar and 1 cup (240 ml) hot water.

Skein Length 40 feet (12 m).

First Dye Pattern Lengths 36" (91.5 cm) very hot pink; 36" (91.5 cm) raven; 72" (183 cm) blueberry; 72" (183 cm) blueberry dashes 2" (5 cm) long with 2" (5-cm) spaces in between; 36" (91.5 cm) blueberry; 36" (91.5 cm) very hot pink; 36" (91.5 cm) maize; 36" (91.5 cm) very hot pink; 36" (91.5 cm) raven; remainder blueberry.

Second Dye Colors Paint the spaces between the blueberry dashes, alternating very hot pink and maize.

Thumb gusset: Knit 6 rnds. Cont as foll:

Rnd 1: (Inc rnd) M1 (see Glossary, page 100), k1, M1, pm, knit to end—46 (50, 54, 58) sts; 3 gusset sts between markers.

Rnd 2: Knit.

Rnd 3: (Inc rnd) M1, knit to next m, M1, slip marker, knit to end—2 sts inc'd between markers.

Rnd 4: Knit.

Rep the last 2 rnds 8 (9, 10, 11) more times—64 (70, 76, 82) sts; 21 (23, 25, 27) gusset sts between markers; piece should measure about 4¾ (5, 5¼, 5½)" (12 [12.5, 13.5, 14] cm) from beg.

Hand: Place 21 (23, 25, 27) gusset sts on a stitch holder (or divide sts on 2 safety pins to make it easier to try on the glove) to work later for thumb, use the backward loop method (see Glossary, page 99) to CO 1 st over the gap, knit to end—44 (48, 52, 56) sts. Knit 6 (8, 8, 8) rnds even, or until piece measures ¾" (1.9 cm) less than desired finished length. *Next rnd:* *K2, p2; rep from * around. Rep the last rnd 5 more times—6 rnds of ribbing completed.

Rolled edge: Knit 5 rnds even. BO all sts loosely. Top edge will roll to outside of glove.

Thumb: Arrange the 21 (23, 25, 27) held gusset sts as evenly as possible on 3 dpn. Join yarn to end of sts with RS facing. Pick up and knit 1 st from base of the st CO over the gap in the hand, knit to end—22 (24, 26, 28) sts. Knit 3 rnds even, inc 2 (0, 2, 0) sts evenly in last rnd—24 (24, 28, 28) sts. *Next rnd:* *K2, p2; rep from * around. Rep the last rnd 4 more times—5 rnds of ribbing completed.

Rolled edge: Knit 5 rnds even. BO all sts loosely. Weave in ends.

Carnival Colors Gloves

What a difference swapping dye colors can make! Hot pink predominates in these gloves, in place of the blue that's most visible in the Carnival Colors Fingerless Gloves (page 91). If you love the yellow, and want it to be most apparent, you could swap it in, instead.

Finished Size 5 (5½, 6, 6½)" (12.5 [14, 15, 16.5] cm) around unstretched, and about 7¾ (10, 10¼, 10½)" (19.5 [25.5, 26, 26.5] cm) long from bottom of cuff to tip of middle finger. To fit child (women's small, women's medium, women's large). *Note:* These gloves are sized for a very snug fit.

Yarn Any off-white, *sock- or fingering-weight* yarn (100% wool or wool/nylon blend), about 200–225 yd (180–205 m).

Needles Set of four double-pointed needles (dpn) size 2 (2.75 mm). Adjust needle size if necessary to obtain the correct gauge.

Notions Tapestry needle; stitch markers; 12 safety pins.

Gauge 35 sts and 46 rnds = 4" (10 cm) in St st.

Gloves (make 2)
Work cuff and thumb gusset as for Carnival Colors Fingerless Gloves on page 91—64 (70, 76, 82) sts; 21 (23, 25, 27) sts between markers; piece measures about 4¾ (5, 5¼, 5½)" (12 [12.5, 13.5, 14] cm) from beg. **Hand:** Place the first 21 (23, 25, 27) sts for thumb on 2 safety

Dye-Pattern Palette Fair Isle #6

very hot pink   blueberry   maize   raven

Dye as for Carnival Colors Fingerless Gloves on page 91, exchanging the blueberry and hot pink colors (paint the blueberry sections with hot pink, and vice-versa).

pins, CO 1 st over the gap, knit to end—44 (48, 52, 56) sts. Work even in St st (knit all sts every rnd) for 1 (2, 2, 2)" (2.5 [5, 5, 5] cm), or until glove reaches to the base of the little finger. Divide sts on 2 needles, 22 (24, 26, 28) sts on each needle; the thumb should be sticking out to the side directly below the space between the needles. Working with the sts on one needle, and beg at the opposite side of the glove from the thumb, place 6 (6, 6, 7) sts on safety pin for pinky, place the next 5 (5, 6, 6) sts on safety pin for ring finger, place the next 5 (6, 6, 7) sts on safety pin for middle finger, and place the rem 6 (7, 8, 8) sts on safety pin for index finger. Rep for the other needle, making sure to beg at the pinky side of the hand. **Index finger:** Transfer 12 (14, 16, 16) sts for index finger from safety pins to dpn. Divide as evenly as possible on 3 needles. Join yarn to end of sts with RS facing. Using the backward loop method (see Glossary, page 99), CO 2 sts over the space between the index and middle fingers, knit to end—14 (16, 18, 18) sts. Work even in St st until index finger measures 1½ (2½, 2½, 3)" (3.8 [6.5, 6.5, 7.5] cm), or about ¼" (0.6 cm) less than desired length. *Next rnd:* *K2tog; rep from * around—7 (8, 9, 9) sts. Work 1 rnd even. *Next rnd:* *K2tog; rep from * around, ending k1 (0, 1, 1)—4 (4, 5, 5) sts. Cut yarn, leaving a 12"

(30.5-cm) tail. Thread tail on tapestry needle and draw through the rem sts. Pull snugly to close fingertip, and fasten off on inside. **Middle finger:** Transfer 10 (12, 12, 14) sts for middle finger from safety pins to dpn. Divide as evenly as possible on 3 needles. Join yarn to end of sts with RS facing. Pick up and knit 4 sts from 2 cast-on sts at base of index finger, knit to end—14 (16, 16, 18) sts. Work even in St st until middle finger measures 1¾ (2¾, 2¾, 3)" (4.5 [7, 7, 7.5] cm), or about ¼" (0.6 cm) less than desired length. *Next rnd:* *K2tog; rep from * around—7 (8, 8, 9) sts. Work 1 rnd even. *Next rnd:* *K2tog; rep from * around, ending k1 (0, 0, 1)—4 (4, 4, 5) sts. Finish as for index finger. **Ring finger:** Transfer 10 (10, 12, 12) sts for ring finger from safety pins to dpn. Divide as evenly as possible on 3 needles. Join yarn to end of sts with RS facing. Pick up and knit 4 sts from base of middle finger, knit to end—14 (14, 16, 16) sts. Work even in St st until middle finger measures 1¾ (2¾, 2¾, 3)" (4.5 [7, 7, 7.5] cm), or about ¼" (0.6 cm) less than desired length. *Next rnd:* *K2tog; rep from * around—7 (7, 8, 8) sts. Work 1 rnd even. *Next rnd:* *K2tog; rep from * around, ending k1 (1, 0, 0)—4 (4, 4, 4) sts. Finish as for index finger. **Pinky:** Transfer 12 (12, 12, 14) sts for pinky from safety pins to dpn. Divide as evenly as possible on 3 needles. Join yarn to end of sts with RS facing. Pick up and knit 2 sts from base of ring finger, knit to end—14 (14, 14, 16) sts. Work even in St st until pinky measures 1¼ (2, 2, 2½)" (3.2 [5, 5, 6.5] cm), or about ¼" (0.6 cm) less than desired length. *Next rnd:* *K2tog; rep from *

around—7 (7, 7, 8) sts. Work 1 rnd even. *Next rnd:* *K2tog; rep from * around, ending k1 (1, 1, 0)—4 (4, 4, 4) sts. Finish as for index finger. Weave in ends, using tails from beg of fingers to close any gaps at the base of the fingers. **Thumb:** Arrange the 21 (23, 25, 27) held gusset sts as evenly as possible on 3 dpn. Join yarn to end of sts with RS facing. Pick up and knit 1 st from base of the st CO over the gap in the hand, knit to end—22 (24, 26, 28) sts. Work even in St st until thumb measures 1 (1½, 1½, 1¾)" (2.5 [3.8, 3.8, 4.5] cm). Cont as foll:

Rnd 1: *K2tog; rep from * around—11 (12, 13, 14) sts rem.

Rnd 2: Knit.

Rnd 3: *K2tog; rep from * around, ending k1 (0, 1, 0)—6 (6, 7, 7) sts rem.

Cut yarn, leaving a 12" (30.5-cm) tail. Thread tail on tapestry needle and draw through the rem sts. Pull snugly to close tip of thumb, and fasten off on inside. Weave in ends.

Carnival Colors Wristbands

We used leftover yarn from other Carnival Colors projects for these wristbands, but you can make fashionable use of leftover finger-ing-weight yarns from other projects, too. If you've knitted many socks with self-pattern-ing yarns, you probably already have a stash at hand that could be put to use.

Finished Size About 6 (8)" (15 [20.5] cm) wrist circumference and 1½" (3.8 cm) wide (both sizes). To fit child (adult).

Yarn *Sock- or fingering-weight wool or wool/nylon blend:* about 40 yd (37 m) off-white per wristband. We used stash yarn.

Dye-Pattern Palette as for Fair Isle #5 and Fair Isle #6

very hot pink	blueberry	maize	raven

If you're using new yarn, dye as for Carnival Colors Fingerless Gloves on page 91 or as for Carnival Colors Gloves, page 93.

Needles Size 2 (2.75 mm): set of 4 double-pointed (dpn). Adjust needle size if necessary to obtain the correct gauge.

Notions Stitch marker (m); tapestry needle.

Gauge 35 sts and 46 rnds = 4" (10 cm) in St st worked in the round.

> *Which stitch patterns show off Fair Isle self-patterning yarns?*
> Garter stitch
> Stockinette stitch
> Reverse stockinette stitch
> All-over ribbing

Stockinette Wristband

CO 52 (70) sts. Divide sts as evenly as possible on 3 dpn. Join for working in the rnd and place marker (pm) to indicate beg of rnd (slip marker every rnd). Work even in St st (knit all sts every rnd) until piece measures 3" (7.5 cm) from beg. BO all sts. With yarn threaded on a tapestry needle, sew CO and BO edges tog with knit side of fabric on the outside. Fold wristband so that the seam is centered on the inside of the band. Weave in ends.

Reverse Stockinette Stitch Wristband

Work as for Stockinette Wristband, sewing CO and BO edges tog so that the purl side of the fabric is on the outside.

Vertical Tube Wristband

CO 28 sts. Divide sts as evenly as possible on 3 dpn. Join for working in the rnd and place marker (pm) to indicate beg of rnd (slip marker every rnd). Work even in St st (knit all sts every rnd) until piece measures 6 (8)" (16.5 [20.5] cm) from beg. BO all sts. With yarn threaded on a tapestry needle, sew CO and BO edges tog with knit side of fabric on the outside of the band. Weave in ends.

carnival colors wristbands

Resources for Yarns and Dyes

Contact the companies listed below if you are unable to find a local retailer or mail-order source for your supplies.

Berroco, Inc.
14 Elmdale Rd.
PO Box 367
Uxbridge, MA 01569-0367
(508) 278-2527
www.berroco.com
Mohair Classic, Pleasure

Brown Sheep Co.
100662 County Rd. 16
Mitchell, NE 69357
(308) 635-2198
www.brownsheep.com
Nature Spun Sport, Nature Spun Worsted, Wildfoote Luxury Sock Yarn

Cartwright's Sequins
11108 N. Hwy. 348
Mountainsburg, AR 72946
www.ccartwright.com

Cascade Yarns
1224 Andover Park East
Tukwila, WA 98188
(206) 574-0440
www.cascadeyarns.com
109 Tweed LE

G & K Craft Industries
PO Box 38
Somerset, MA 02726
(508) 676-3883
Country Classics Dyes

Henry's Attic
5 Mercury Ave.
Monroe, NY 10950
(845) 783-3930
Montana 4/8 Wool

Ironstone Yarns
PO Box 8
Las Vegas, NM 87701
(800) 343-4914
English Mohair

JCA, Inc./Reynolds
35 Scales Ln.
Townsend, MA 01469
(800) 225-6340
Alafoss Lopi

Kreinik Manufacturing Co.
3106 Lord Baltimore Dr., Ste. 101
Baltimore, MD 21244
(800) 537-2166
www.kreinik.com
Kreinik Metallics Balger Cord

Louet Sales
In United States:
808 Commerce Park Dr.
Ogdensburg, NY 13669
In Canada:
3425 Hands Rd.
Prescott, ON, Canada K0E 1T0
(613) 925-4502
www.louet.com
Gaywool Dyes

Meilke's Farm Fiber Arts
2550 Co. Rd. II
Rudolph, WI 54475-9409
(715) 344-4104
www.meilkesfarm.com
Country Classics Dyes

Mission Falls
In United States:
Unique Kolours
28 North Bacton Hill Rd.
Malvern, PA 19355
(800) 252-3934
www.uniquekolours.com
In Canada:
PO Box 224
Consecon, ON, Canada K0K 1T0
www.missionfalls.com
Mission Falls 1824 Cotton

Patons/Spinrite
320 Livingstone Ave. South
Listowel, ON, Canada N4W 3H3
(519) 291-3780
www.patonsyarns.com
Classic Merino Wool

Phoenix Brands, LLC—CPC Specialty Markets USA
PO Box 21070
Indianapolis, IN 46221
(866) 794-0800
www.ritdye.com
Rit Dyes

Abbreviations List

beg	beginning, begin(s)
BO	bind off
cir	circular needle
cm	centimeter
cn	cable needle
CO	cast on
cont	continue(s)
dpn	double-pointed needles
foll	following, follow(s)
g	gram(s)
K, k	knit
kwise	as if to knit
m	meter(s)
M1	make 1 (an increase)
ml	milliliter(s)

P, p	purl
patt	pattern(s)
psso	pass slipped stitch over
pwise	as if to purl
rem	remain(s)
rep	repeat(s)
rnd(s)	round(s)
RS	right side
st(s)	stitch(es)
St st	stockinette stitch: knit all sts on right side, purl all sts on wrong side
tog	together
WS	wrong side
yd	yard(s)

GLOSSARY

Attached I-Cord

As I-cord is knitted, attach it to the garment as follows: With garment RS facing and using a separate ball of yarn and circular needle, pick up the desired number of stitches along the garment edge. Slide these stitches down the needle so that the first picked-up stitch is near the opposite needle point. With double-pointed needle, cast on desired number of I-cord stitches. Knit across the I-cord to the last stitch, then knit the last stitch together with the first picked-up stitch on the garment, and pull the yarn behind the cord. Knit to the last I-cord stitch, then knit the last I-cord stitch together with the next picked-up stitch. Continue in this manner until all picked-up stitches have been used.

I-Cord

With double-pointed needle, cast on desired number of stitches. *Without turning the needle, slide the stitches to other end of the needle, pull the yarn around the back, and knit the stitches as usual; repeat from * for desired length.

Backward Loop Cast-On

*Loop working yarn and place it on needle backward so that it doesn't unwind. Repeat from *.

Continental (Long-Tail) Cast-On

Leaving a long tail (about ½" to 1" [1.3 to 2.5 cm] for each stitch to be cast on), make a slipknot and place on right needle. Place thumb and index finger of left hand between yarn ends so that working yarn is around index finger and tail end is around thumb. Secure ends with your other fingers and hold palm upwards, making a V of yarn (Figure 1). Bring needle up through loop on thumb (Figure 2), grab first strand around index finger with needle, and go back down through loop on thumb (Figure 3). Drop loop off thumb and, placing thumb back in V configuration, tighten resulting stitch on needle (Figure 4).

Figure 1   *Figure 2*   *Figure 3*   *Figure 4*

Kitchener Stitch

Step 1: Bring threaded needle through front stitch as if to purl and leave stitch on needle.

Step 2: Bring threaded needle through back stitch as if to knit and leave stitch on needle.

Step 3: Bring threaded needle through same front stitch as if to knit and slip this stitch off needle. Bring threaded needle through next front stitch as if to purl and leave stitch on needle.

Step 4: Bring threaded needle through first back stitch as if to purl (as illustrated), slip this stitch off, bring needle through next back stitch as if to knit, leave this stitch on needle. Repeat Steps 3 and 4 until no stitches remain on needles.

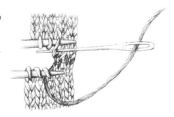

Mattress Stitch Seam

With RS of knitting facing, use threaded needle to pick up one bar between first two stitches on one piece (Figure 1), then corresponding bar plus the bar above it on other piece (Figure 2). *Pick up next two bars on first piece, then next two bars on the other piece (Figure 3). Repeat from * to end of seam, finishing by picking up last bar (or pair of bars) at the top of first piece.

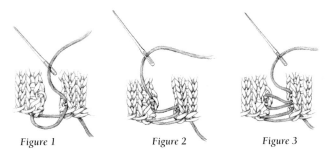

Figure 1   *Figure 2*   *Figure 3*

Niddy-Noddy

To use a niddy-noddy, hold the yarn end against the center shaft with one hand. Use your other hand to guide the yarn around the four arms as follows (rotate the niddy-noddy by moving your wrist as necessary): *Guide the yarn up and over the arm to the right, down and under the arm to the back, up and over the arm to the left, then down and under the arm in front (Figures 1 and

Figure 1

glossary

2). Repeat from * until all of the yarn has been used, maintaining constant tension throughout. Use the two ends of the yarn to tie knots around the skein (Figure 3), then slip the skein off the niddy-noddy.

Figure 2

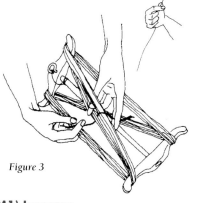

Figure 3

Raised (M1) Increase

With left needle tip, lift strand between needles from front to back (Figure 1). Knit lifted loop through the back (Figure 2).

Figure 1   *Figure 2*

Single Crochet (sc)

Insert hook into an edge stitch, yarn over hook and draw a loop through stitch, yarn over hook (Figure 1) and draw it through both loops on hook (Figure 2).

Figure 1   *Figure 2*

Slip-Stitch Crochet (sl st)

Insert hook into stitch, yarn over hook and draw loop through stitch and loop on hook.

Three-Needle Bind-Off

Place stitches to be joined onto two separate needles. Hold them with right sides of knitting facing together. Insert a third needle into first stitch on each of the other two needles and knit them together as one stitch. *Knit next stitch on each needle the same way. Pass first stitch over second stitch. Repeat from * until one stitch remains on third needle. Cut yarn and pull tail through last stitch.

INDEX

101

abbreviations 98

band depth 9, 10
bands, graduated 12, 18, 22–25
    monochrome 25
        dye palette #1 33
        dye palette #2 37
    multicolor 25
        dye palette #1 39
        dye palette #2 43
        dye palette #3 45
    projects 30–47
bind-off 100

cast-on 99
color palettes 29
    dye palette Fair Isle #1 29
    dye palette monochrome #1 33
    dye palette monochrome #2 37
    dye palette multicolor #1 39
    dye palette multicolor #2 43
    dye palette multicolor #3 45
color
adjustment 75
satisfaction 26, 41
Country Classics dye 15
crochet 100

dashes 21
dyeing
    heat-setting 26
    immersion 22–25, 26
dye lots 28
dyes 14, 15
    absorbtion 20
    handpainting 18, 20
    immersion 18
    mixing 19
    union 15

embellishments 35
equipment 16–17

Fair Isle 9, 12, 13, 18, 21

dye palette #1 29, 73
dye palette #2 75
dye palette #3 77, 81
dye palette #4 83, 85
dye palette #5 87, 91
dye palette #6 93, 96
projects 70–97

Gaywood dye 15
glossary 99

handpainting dyes 18, 19
heat-setting dyes 26, 27, 28

I-cord 99
immersion dyes 18
increase 100

Kitchener stitch 99

mattress stitch 99
microwaves 26, 27

niddy-noddy 22, 24, 99, 100

pattern adjustments 90
projects
    Asymmetrical Vest 86–90
    Autumn Sparkle Mittens, Headband, and Scarf 39–41
    Autumn Stripes Socks 66–67
    Carnival Colors Fingerless Gloves 91–92
    Carnival Colors Gloves 93–95
    Carnival Colors Wristbands 96–97
    Child's Watermelon Sweater and Socks 60–63
    Cool Blues Summer Shell 50–52
    Cute as a Button hat, mittens, and scarf 32–35
    Forest Trail Socks 72–73
    Garden Colors Pillow Tops 53–55
    Harbor Lights Leg Warmer Set 56–57
    Ladies' Watermelon Socks 64–65

Keyhole Scarf 80–81
Midnight Garden Socks 74–75
No-Slip Slipper Socks 76–79
School's Out Summer Shell 45–47
Spring Stripes Socks 68–69
Tassel-Top Earflap Hats 82–83, 84
Wee Winter Mittens 84–85
Wine-Stained Cables Hat and Scarf 42–44
Winter Frost Hat and Mittens 36–38

resources 98
Rit dye 15

self patterning defined 9, 10
skeins 10–11, 12, 19
    winding into balls 28, 29
slipper soles 79
steam-setting dyes 27
stitches 99–100
stitch patterns 47, 55, 69, 97
stripes 9, 10, 12, 20, 21
    dye palette #1 61, 65
    dye palette #2 67
    dye palette #3 69
    projects 58–69

utensils see equipment

winding objects 10, 11
workspace, preparing 19

yarn
    care 13
    pattern matching 67
    selecting 15
    shortage 12
    winding 10–12

zigzags 9, 10, 12, 18, 21, 22
    dye palette #1 51
    dye palette #2 53
    dye palette #3 57
    projects 48–57

Index

NOTES

NOTES

NOTES